101 Healthy Meals In 5 Minutes or Less

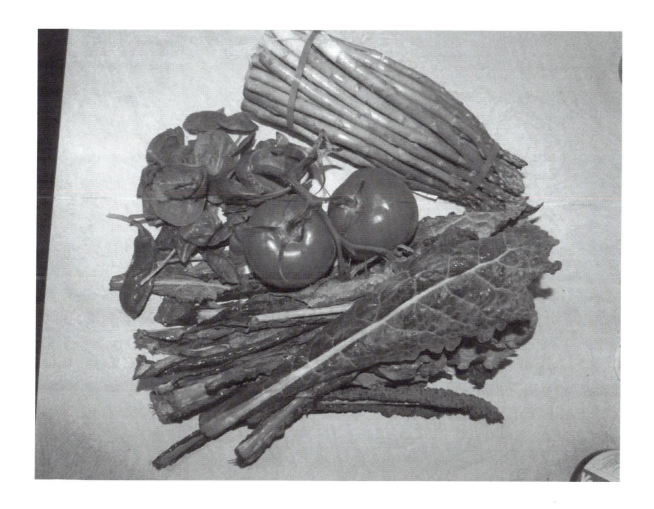

Victoria C. Leo, MA

Complete programs, classes, retreats
www.soaringdragon.biz
Find me on Facebook, Linked In, Pinterest, others
Victoria C Leo

101 Healthy Meals

All text and photographs copyright Victoria C. Leo, 2012. All rights reserved.

THE AUTHOR WORKED HARD, FOR MONTHS, TO CREATE THIS. MAKING COPIES IS STEALING. YOU WOULDN'T WANT SOMEONE TO RIP YOU OFF, WOULD YOU? LET FRIENDS BUY THEIR OWN COPIES. DO THE RIGHT THING.

Contact the author at:
Soar With the Eagles
www.soaringreiki.com
253.203.6676
Victoria@soaringreiki.com

Dedicated to the memory of my inspiring adoptive mother, **Elizabeth Pearson**, who succeeded in teaching me that the stove isn't so scary after all, and that the kitchen can be my friend. She also taught me how to follow a recipe without ad-libbing, and very occasionally I do in fact cook that way. The ad-lib DNA cannot be gainsaid, however. My biological ancestors were all intuitive, right-brained cooks or musicians and I can't seem to stop going off the rails. Sorry, mom. You tried.

And to my darling husband and life partner, **Rick Baird**, who thinks that I'm a great cook and (oh, dear Lord), says so in public to actual people. You can see it as delusional. I see a faith so strong, so complete, that it overpowers all rational evidence to the contrary. While I appreciate and laud the role of reason and evidence in science, I know the equally-critical role of faith in human lives, and the extent to which I've been blessed by this relationship, on so many levels, takes my breath away. What wondrous love is this, oh, my soul, oh, my soul.

Who is this book for?

Well, not professional cooks. Not people who regularly buy and use cookbooks. They don't care about prep time. No, this book is for harried and only marginally masterful folks who consider cooking a bit of creative anarchy – or a thankless chore - on the road to getting healthy nutrition into themselves and their families in the smallest amount of time possible.

Maybe you're a busy career person, with a family to cook for at the end of a long day. Perhaps you've been cooking for yourself or a family long enough that the thrill is gone and you just want to get through the chore as fast as possible. If you are in the latter category, this cookbook may re-spark your creative juices, and help you to fall in love with the creation of a healthy meal. Or not. I feel your pain, brothers and sisters.

This cookbook is also for people who like variety, because these recipes are designed for you to mix and match. Just don't put lemon and cinnamon in the same dish. Ever. Trust me.

What will you get if you take this book home?

The title promises fast. You can get any of these meals or snacks put together in 5 minutes or less. [This is your prep time. When the oven is working, you can go take care of the kids or read a book.] It might take you a bit more prep the first time, as you may be tentative, need to read instructions twice or not know what a word means. I don't use much fancy kitchen vocab because I don't know much fancy kitchen vocab, but it could happen. If you don't know what "sauté" means, Google it. There's probably a YouTube video as well. If you've never used a knife and a zucchini in the same sentence, it might take you a minute or so more to practice not slicing your fingers off.

It also promises healthy. So let's define what "healthy" means. I have Master's degrees in Biology and in Psychology. I know all about nutrition and I know how you (yes, you) think and feel and make excuses and tell yourself stories to try to make apple pie a "fruit" on the nutrition chart. Uh, huh. It ain't gonna work with me, so be warned: this is the Total Truth Zone.

We learn our foodways as children. Food is a bribe. Food is an alternative to the love that we don't get, the attention that we need and our adult guardians can't or won't give us. We reward ourselves with what "tastes good," because this is our primary language of love. We were taught that you eat to show you love, you eat to show solidarity with the ethnic clan, you eat because you're lonely and unloved, you eat because you're frustrated, blocked from getting your needs met and stressed from over-work and under-play-and-rest.

Food in this industrial culture is almost never about what it's supposed to be about. Food is supposed to be about nutrition. It's supposed to be about health, full stop.

Food = health

One of the problems that people habitually have when they decide that they want to live a longer, healthy life (which good nutrition vastly increases your chances of, by vastly reducing your probability of getting cancer, heart disease and diabetes) is that they use the wrong criteria.

People demand that the new food taste as "good" as what they are used to eating.

And it can't. Not immediately, anyway.

When people talk about "tasty" what they mean is high levels of fat, sugar, salt and umami. You have receptors for all of these substances on your tongue and they are connected to the Reward center in your brain. When the Reward center gets an incoming neuronal signal, it releases dopamine. This is the chemical that makes you feel like you're flying high, "in love," "good" and all things bright and beautiful. It's why addicts feel their hit after taking cocaine or you, not technically an addict, feel when you slip some chocolate into your day. Dopamine high! Woo-hoo! Umami, if you haven't Googled it already, is the "savory" flavor that people crave when they say they crave meat; it's caused by the molecule *glutamate*. It's also in most cheeses, and in carrots, which is why more people like carrot juice than any other kind of veggie juice. Of course you love the taste of meat and cheese. Your umami sensors are connected to a dopamine releaser!

Millions of years ago, before your ancestors were *Homo sapiens,* one of those lucky guys or gals was born with a mutation in their DNA that gave them an umami sensor. Suddenly they were enjoying the dopamine hit from eating the infrequent scavenged meat that they found, or a pal found. They started looking for more meat. They started thinking about trapping some little critters that they could turn into dinner or scavenging shellfish. Another ancestor had a DNA screw loose and popped into existence with a weird taste for fat. S/he started looking for fats and oils in the forest and savanna.

Those two mutations changed our ancestors profoundly, and their descendants were the ones who survived to be you and me. Meat, although we don't need to consume it now, was essential for our ancestors back then. Eating animals, fish and other river and lake critters as well as land animals, gave our ancestors more protein in their diet and the good fats that they needed, both for the same purpose – to sustain a 50% increase in brain size. With a bigger brain, our Homo erectus ancestors created the first real language (we could communicate about the past and future; we could make plans and explain concepts, not just our immediate emotional condition, which is all most animal communication is). They tamed fire. This meant that they were protected from predators and could sleep peacefully at night for the first time in 6 million years. They could cook their food, which meant that they got more nutrition from their food. [Raw plant food leaves a lot of nutrition undigested, one reason why modern raw food diets help you lose weight.] Babies and elders had better nutrition because the cooked food was softer. Cooking was major. (Read Catching

Fire, by an anthropologist, for more on this.) They set up home bases so the more slowly-maturing babies could be cared for. Elders could be cared for as well, and their stored wisdom and knowledge mined for group survival. That was the beginning of the road that led to Homo sapiens. SO we can't say that we're sorry that we have these umami (protein, mostly) and fat sensors in our tongues and our brains, because they were essential for the evolution of the human species. BUT – they are a big, big, BIG problem today – arguably the biggest problem in modern nutrition and health.

It means that **you cannot – absolutely cannot – let "it tastes good" be your criterion for whether you eat something or not**.

Why? Because if you do, you are a manipulated puppet in the hands of the food corporations, who know that you have this dopamine pathway in your brain and will fill their products with as much fat, sugar, salt and umami as they can, regardless of what the consequences are for you.

If you get diabetes in your thirties, or cancer in your forties, this is a disaster for you, your family, and your country. A healthy citizenry is a strategic resource and Americans are a lot less healthy than Europeans, Canadians and practically everyone else on Earth who doesn't live in the Third World. It is not a disaster for the corporations that kill you or turn you into a stroke-disabled invalid way too young. They have your money, which is all they care about. But it is a disaster for your family and your country. We need you strong and healthy, to build and contribute 100%.

So, it's up to you to protect yourself, from yourself. Your thinking brain – your executive functions in the prefrontal cortex, right behind your forehead – needs to be in charge, and you need to be willing to commit to **FOOD = HEALTH** for at least 30 days. Within that period, if you go cold-turkey, your body will adjust to the New Normal. Even your taste buds will adjust. Small amounts of sugar, fat and umami will taste "good." You will be able to enjoy your meals as you pursue health.

Just don't think you're cured. As long as you're alive and a human being, that Reward center will be lurking, ready to give you a jolt of dopamine and get you addicted to that jolt again. It's more like being on the wagon for alcohol abuse. You can never totally relax your vigilance. A recovered alcoholic is just one drink away from a bender. You have to stay away from the high-fat, high-umami, high-salt, high-sugar aisle. If you make exceptions – weddings, Christmas, the Dalai Lama's birthday party, etc. – just make sure that you realize that you have probably re-activated your cravings and will need to be super-vigilant for the next 30 days.

If you have family and friends who try to guilt-trip you into equating food with love or family identity, gently and repeatedly say "Doctor's orders" and step away from the stuff that doesn't lead to health. Love isn't encapsulated in Swedish meatballs or coconut crème pie. Shine that love light in your eyes, smile like the Buddha or Jesus, and do what you know is right for your health. If these folks will cry buckets at your funeral but don't want to help you postpone that date as long as possible, they don't define love the way I do, and you need to decide for yourself what kind of love you want for yourself. I eat before I go to see the *love=fattyfood* crowd so I'm not hungry when I get there. Doctor's orders, doctor's orders, doctor's orders, amen. See my book Take Back Your Lost Heart for more ideas.

If you work long hours and come home hungry

101 Healthy Meals

Prepare ahead of time. Make large portions and box up half of it for tomorrow. Bake several meals worth on Sunday. Each prep takes 5 minutes. Intersperse it with your ball games or whatever. If you wait until you are exhausted and starved, even 5 minutes of prep will feel like Too Much. Be realistic.

Make whole-wheat pasta in advance. Make big batches of brown rice. Then eat different pasta or rice dishes for several days.

101 Healthy Meals

Table of Contents

Recipe List

Section 0: Getting Started
This is where you learn what to stock your fridge and pantry with, and what the ingredients mean.

Section 1: Stir fry, Baked entrees & Burritos/Wraps
These are things that you are going to stir-fry in olive oil, or toss into a glass baking dish, or put onto a tortilla or put into a wrap, or use to make pizza. Veggie sausage. More baked goodness that you ever knew existed.

Section 2: Soups, Stew, Skewers or Pasta
Soup as a side or a meal, stews that make different meals all winter long, putting cool stuff on a skewer and broiling it, and making pasta of all sorts.

Section 3: Eating Vegetables, Eating Fruit, Eating Whole Grains & Legumes
You know that most of what you need to eat every day is vegetables and there are a lot of veggies in the other sections. Learn more about veggies, fruit, legumes and whole grains and explore some additional recipes.

Section 4: Breakfast
If you want to lose weight, have energy, think straight and be kind to your cat, you absolutely must get protein into your body within two hours of getting out of bed. These are painless.

Section 5: Healthy Desserts
Call these treats and enjoy. Easy, fast and good for you.

Section 6: All the Stuff That Doesn't Fit in the Other Categories…. Including Seasonal Holiday Dishes

Lots of good stuff here…. From healthy snacks to salads to Thanksgiving options

Moving on From 5 Minute Health

Author Bio & Interview

Coupon Offer

101 Healthy Meals

List of Recipes:

1> Veggie Stir Fry	**Starting Sec 3**
	55> Veggies & Seafood
2> Fake Meat Stir Fry	56> Fish & Rice
3> Real Meat Stir Fry	57> Spaghetti Squash & Leftovers
4> Seafood Stir Fry	58-59> Sweet Potatoes/Yams
5-8> Stir Fry with Pasta Sauce	60> Grilled Greens
9-12> Stir Fry with Cheese	61-64> Portobello Mushrooms
13> Wok	65-69> Tempeh
14> Healthy Pizza	70> Garbanzo & Cucumber Salad
15> Mini-Pizzas	71> Fruit & Cucumber Yogurt Salad
16> Baked Mac and Cheese	**Starting Sec 4**
	72-75> Scrambled Eggs/Omelets
17-19> Lasagna	76> Huevos Rancheros
20> Leftovers & Frozen Veggies Casserole	77> French Toast
21-22> Fish Bakes	78> Healthy Cereal Meals
23> Salad Shrimp Bake	79> Protein with Russet Potatoes
24> Jumbo Shrimp Bake	80-81> Smoothies
25> Scallops Bake	82> Breakfast parfait
26-27> Crab Bakes	**Starting Section 5**
	83> Dessert Parfait
28-30> Sausage Bakes	84> High Protein Pumpkin Pie
31> Quesadilla	85> Lassi, Skyr, Ethnic Delights
32-34> Meat & Rice Casseroles	86> Nut Butter & Celery
35-36> Tomatoes & Veg Chicken w/Brown Rice	87> Melons With Filling
37> Veg Burrito	88-89> Fruit Pies
38> Meat Burrito	90> High Protein Muffins
39> Eggplant Parmigiana	**Starting Section 6**
	91-92 Nachos
40> Carrots	93> Acorn Squash w/Yogurt & Peppers
41> Asparagus & Fish	94> Veggies & Veg Chicken for Holidays
42> Stuffed Peppers	95> Hummus
Starting Sec 2	96> Open Face Sandwiches
43> Seafood Soup/Stew	
44> Split Pea	97> Steamed Holiday Veggies
45> Lentil	98> Seafood/Protein Salad
46> 3 Bean	99> Mashed Squash for the Holidays
47> Vegetable	100> Holiday Dinner Overview
48> Veggie Dog Soup/Stew	101> Eating Out w/a Plan
49> Asparagus & Onion	
50> Seafood Pasta/Meatballs	
51-52> Primavera/Meatballs	
53> Get Skewered!	
54> Grill the Night Away	

Section 0: Getting Started

This is what you need to own. Go get them. I'll wait.

1. a good no-stick frying pan. If you like cast-iron and seasoning the dang thing and fussing over it, god bless you and go ahead. If not, sit down here beside me. You can survive without it.

2. several glass baking dishes. Get a small dish and a large dish. I prefer the Goldilocks-style and have three sizes, but two will do you.

3. some bamboo skewers.

4. dinner-size bowls (makes the meal look bigger because it climbs higher)

Highly recommended:
- a spoon with colander in place of the spoon or a full-size colander;
- microwave oven.

Anything you don't own you can get easily. Bowls and glass baking dishes are a staple at thrift stores. Get your pans new.

Spices, Sauces, Vitamins, Micronutrients, Vinegar & Olive Oil

You must own lots and lots of olive oil and you must use it with every meal except ice cream. A key component of the Mediterranean Diet that has been shown to lower rates of every health problem except flat feet, olive oil gives you lots of good fats. Don't run out. Use Benecol and other healthy butter substitutes for your toast, but use olive oil for all cooking, baking and salads. Other oils try to act as good as olive oil, but nothing beats the Real Stuff.

Check out all the fancy-tasting vinegars out there. If you have a really sinfully delish vinegar, a salad tastes great. Really. It also makes a great marinade for the bland-tasting veggies. They pick up the pizazz of the vinegar after just 5 minutes of soaking.

Take a quality multi-vitamin every day. If you live where the winter is dark and overcast and lasts more than two months, increase your Vitamin D to at least 1200 units/day (or whatever your MD, ARNP, Naturopathic Physician or other licensed medical professional says), from dairy or from a supplement. People always over-estimate how much good stuff they are eating. You probably are, too. Take a supplement during the dark months. Take magnesium and calcium. You can get calcium in candy form, in a supplement or from powders. You probably aren't getting enough from your diet.

If you are prone to winter "blues" get my book Journey Out of SAD: Beat the Winter Blues NOW!, from the publisher (www.lulu.com), or from Amazon. It's even available as a Kindle book.

In many cases, a basically healthy food is destroyed by slathering it with a high-fat, high-sugar, high-salt sauce. One of the ways that young men, with their ferociously high metabolisms, can shed ten pounds in no time flat is cutting out sauces. This cookbook has only healthy sauces, or it substitutes spice taste for sauce. You don't need sauce.

The sauces in this cookbook are generally of two kinds:

- based on plain, unsweetened yogurt, enlivened with cinnamon (a spice that is known to help you reduce cravings and lose weight – and tastes divine) and other "sweet" spices

- non-existent. The food tastes great with olive oil sprinkled on and lots of spices.

Spices come in two major families:

- sharp tastes like onion, garlic, black pepper and sodium chloride (table salt) substitutes like potassium chloride;

- sweet spices like parsley, rosemary, thyme, marjoram, cinnamon, cardamom and similar tastes.

You need to have lots of spice in your kitchen, for great taste and no calories. Spices led to hundreds of years of war in Europe and Asia, and no wonder. In addition to preserving food, they make ordinary food into paradise. In modern packaged, prepared food, this transformation is done by adding salt that will kill you decades before you should go. With spices, you can have taste – and decades of vibrant LIFE. Hooray!

Where to find taste treats

In the past 150 years, food has stopped being grown by family farmers and is now a product produced purely for profit by corporations. As such, it makes sense for them to choose products that stay fresh longer and resist bruising, rather than food that tastes good or has nutrition. Where do you get veggies and fruits that give you the biggest taste and nutrition bang for your grocery buck?

- *Farmer's markets. Look for "heirloom" veggies.* Buy some. Try them in these recipes. Remember, your brain interprets anything new as "bad" unless it is overwhelmingly sweet or fatty. Give yourself at least two tries before you ditch something. I know, I make your brain sound as sophisticated as the average two-year old's. But that's how it is. Being careful and suspicious kept our ancestors alive, and that's why they lived long enough to have grandchildren, and that's why we are alive today. The gene for food conservatism had its place eight million years ago. Be aware of it and laugh as you remind yourself that this isn't the savanna of long-ago Africa, this is 2012….

- *You can also find plants for sale.* If you don't live in the Puget Sound area, where the growing season is about two weeks long, growing veggies gives you the stress-relief of gardening and the succulent food as a reward. There is nothing on this earth as mouth-wateringly wonderful as a carrot fresh from the ground. That or an organic young carrot at a Farmer's Market or other outlet will make you swoon like you did in high school over your first love.

101 Healthy Meals

- *Farmer's markets are also a good place to find new fruits.*

- *Ethnic groceries.* Most proprietors are happy to explain things. Take the kids and make it a family outing or leave them with their other parent and make it a quiet, restful time; you know your kids so be honest about what kind of experience it would be. You can find amazing veggies, fruits, grass-fed animal products and whole-grains. You can research anything on the Web. My sister, who was born and raised in Ethiopia, introduced me to teff and I love it for breakfast (see Breakfast section). They sell it in major grocery stores and also health food stores. Quinoa is an amazing grain and there are almost-instant versions of it at health food stores. Asian groceries are particularly good for veggies. East African, Middle-Eastern and Mediterranean cultures have wonderful grain choices.

- *Health food stores frequently have a wider selection of heirloom or at least organic veggies and fruits.* You can find bread that isn't made from flour, just sprouted grain (sooooo yummy) and lots of heirloom grains.

- Many *local farmers are offering a subscription service* where you get a box of what's in season every week for a set fee. If you end up with something that's not covered in this cookbook, just let Google and YouTube guide you through more recipes than there are hours in the day, even for the most obscure stuff.

- *The Web.* You can find anything, order anything. Google "heirloom vegetables" and you'll have your entertainment needs taken care of for the next month. You can get sex toys from Amazon and food delivered to your door from nearly anywhere. Technology has its uses.

Once you have your suppliers set up, it's easy to swing by and stock up regularly. Or you can eat standard boring veggies to save time and have the heirlooms and the ethnic as a taste treat on the weekends.

And remember perhaps the most important key to success in healthy eating, brilliantly explained by my mother in the immortal words, "It's food. Eat it or go to bed hungry." No fussy kids at that house. Fussy is learned behavior. My husband and I have a "Thank you, dear," rule. The cook gets to choose what's for dinner. If you didn't cook, you sit down, chow down and be grateful.

Section 1:
Stir fry, Baked Entrees & Burritos/Wraps

Yes, it's true. This is the biggest section of the book. And why not? It covers a lot of ground!

Stir Frys

All stir-fry's have some elements in common. You lightly-cook your ingredients in a single pan, so you lock in the nutrition. They are quick and easy to do.

For all of them, you start with chopped up or sliced veggies and chopped up or sliced pre-cooked protein. If you go to a grocery store, you can get pre-sliced veggies. If they are organic or uncommon, you may have to chop/slice them yourself.

Baking

Baked dishes are a favorite for 5-minutes-or-less cooks because you throw the ingredients into a glass baking dish and then come back when the timer goes off. Anyone can do it. The joy of all these baked recipes is that they all look and taste so different, yet they all start "life" in the same set of glass baking dishes. Enjoy!

Recipe 1: Veggie Stir Fry

Complete procedure:

1. Prepare veggies. Slice thin or chop in small pieces. I recommend zucchini, carrots (especially if pre-chopped), shredded broccoli if you can get it, spinach, kale, chard.
2. Spray your fry pan with olive oil spray or use a small amount of the oil, making sure the whole pan is covered but not drowning.
3. Put the element on medium heat. As the veggies start to sizzle, lower to medium-low if you have it. Veggies will lose water and cover only half the space they started with, so throw in more veggies than you think you need.
4. Add walnuts, pecans, cashews or peanuts for added protein and good fats.
5. Add sweet or onion family of spices. Use twice as much as you think you need. Better to have a bit more flavor than a bit less, especially your first time.
6. Wait 2 minutes. Flip over the veggies so the other side gets lightly cooked.

Serve with protein-focused soup or salad, with oil [quiz time: what kind of oil?] and vinegar dressing. Drizzle the oil; don't drown the salad.

Recipe 2: Fake Meat Stir Fry

The vegetarian meat substitutes available these days are legion. The fake sliced chickens are very good. If you are willing to go for a heavier dose of fats, you can use the kielbasa, chorizo and Italian sausage. Field roast is pretty good. Tofurkey comes in either the turkey-only and complete-meal versions. I'm too lazy for stuffing, sauce and the whole megilla. [Is it obvious why I'm the guru of Quick?]

Try a whole bunch of them. Come home with twenty. I'm serious. If you hate one, feed it to the dog or rabbit; rabbits will eat anything healthy. If you like one, keep the wrapper or write down the name. We have a dry-erase board on the fridge where we keep running notes for the next shopping trip.

Complete procedure:

1. Prepare veggies. Slice thin or chop in small pieces. I recommend zucchini, carrots (especially if pre-chopped), shredded broccoli if you can get it, spinach, kale, chard.
2. Spray your fry pan with olive oil spray or use a small amount of the oil, making sure the whole pan is covered but not drowning.
3. Put the element on medium heat. As the veggies start to sizzle, lower to medium-low if you have it.
4. Veggies will lose water and cover only half the space they started with, so throw in more veggies than you think you need.
5. Wait 2 minutes. Flip over the veggies so the other side gets lightly cooked.
6. Add the protein.
7. Add walnuts, cashews, pecans or other nuts for more protein and good fats.
8. Add the sweet or onion family of spices. Use twice as much as you think you need. Better to have a bit more flavor than a bit less, especially your first time.
9. Give it another minute or so to brown.

Serve with soup or salad, oil [quiz time: what kind of oil?] and vinegar dressing. Drizzle the oil; don't drown the salad.

Recipe 3: Real Meat Stir Fry

I haven't eaten a dead animal that lived on land in a really long time, so I can't help much here. I recommend that you follow recipe 2.

I recommend that you stay away from "red meat" for a number of health-related reasons. Beef is filled with really high levels of cancer-causing PCBs. It also has a scary-high level of female hormone, which the CDC is looking at for man-boob development and issues of low-sperm count and defective sperm (leads to birth defects in babies) in men as well as cancer in both sexes. It also has sky-high cholesterol and saturated fat levels. You can avoid PCBs and hormones by buying pasture-raised animals, but they tend to have lots more fat. Pork is almost as bad. Chicken and turkey is less harmful to your body, but the poor animals are raised in such hellish conditions, the details would turn a sociopath's stomach.

Give meat substitute a try. Use several different brands before you decide it doesn't taste good. It will taste a little different, but different and bad are only equivalent in the primitive brain levels, remember. Your prefrontal cortex (thinking brain) can figure out the difference.

Recipe 4: Seafood Stir Fry

    There are so many options here:
- **Shrimp (larger size is better)**
- **Fake crab (it's some other kind of fish)**
- **Scallops (they will need more cooking time than my 5 minute limit, more like 8)**
- **Leftover baked fish from last night's dinner**

Complete procedure:

1. Prepare veggies. Slice thin or chop in small pieces. I recommend zucchini, carrots (especially if pre-chopped), shredded broccoli if you can get it, spinach, kale, chard.
2. Spray your fry pan with olive oil spray or use a small amount of the oil, making sure the whole pan is covered but not drowning.
3. Put the element on medium heat. As the veggies start to sizzle, lower to medium-low if you have it.
4. Veggies will lose water and cover only half the space they started with, so throw in more veggies than you think you need.
5. Wait 2 minutes. Flip over the veggies so the other side gets lightly cooked.
6. Add the seafood.
7. Add sweet or onion family of spices. Use twice as much as you think you need. Better to have a bit more flavor than a bit less, especially your first time.
8. Give it another minute or so to brown. More time if it's scallops.

Note on frozen food: Nuke it in the microwave until it's unfrozen. Do this during Step 1 above. Usually 2-3 minutes.

Serve with soup or salad, oil [quiz time: what kind of oil?] and vinegar dressing. Drizzle the oil; don't drown the salad. Don't even think about bleu-cheese, Thousand Island or creamy-anything dressing. I can feel your arteries occluding from here.

Recipes 5-8: Stir Fry with Pasta Sauce

Recipe 5: Veggies only
Recipe 6: Meat Substitute
Recipe 7: Chicken or Turkey
Recipe 8: Seafood

Whether it's the veggies, the fake meat, the real dead animal, or the seafood versions, it basically works the same.

1. Put all the ingredients in the pan at the same time (unfreeze the frozen before you start this).
2. Then go to medium-low, add pasta sauce so that the food is covered but not drowning – less is more here.
3. Set your timer for 5 minutes. Add sweet spices.
4. Come back when it dings. Put it in bowls.
5. Add parmesan cheese - not too much. Parmesan has lots of umami but lots of fat. See if you can find a fake parmesan or use Romano.

Make a quick spinach salad with walnuts and some berries or oranges (OK, be a purist, this adds another 2 minutes).

Recipes 9-12: Stir Fry with Cheese

Recipe 9: Veggies only
Recipe 10: Meat Substitute
Recipe 11: Chicken or Turkey
Recipe 12: Seafood

Whether it's the veggies, the fake meat, the real dead animal, or the seafood versions, it basically works the same.

1. Put all the ingredients in the pan at the same time (unfreeze the frozen before you start this).
2. Then go to medium-low, sprinkle Daiya brand non-dairy cheese so that the food is covered. Daiya melts really nicely. You can also use non-fat or part-skim mozzarella.
3. Set your timer for 5 minutes. Add sweet spices.
4. Come back when it dings. Put it in bowls.
5. Add parmesan cheese - not too much. Parmesan has lots of umami but lots of fat. See if you can find a fake parmesan or use Romano.

Make a quick spinach salad with walnuts and some berries or oranges (OK, be a purist, this adds another 2 minutes).

Recipe 13: Using a Wok for your Stir Fry

I haven't used a wok in about a million years (too lazy to take care of the old-style ones, which are as fussy as cast iron skillets). There are new electric ones that are completely idiot proof. They are nice because you can put veggies in the center to cook and then move them to the outer areas, which are cooler, while something else cooks. I'm not sure you can do this in the 5 minutes I allocate for meal prep, but as you get more experienced and you want to spend more time, this is something to consider. Or not.

Baked Entrees

    Pizza
    Veggie and Protein Casseroles
    Seafood Casseroles
    Italian-style eating
    Quesadillas
    Burritos

Recipe 14: Healthy Pizza

Ordinary pizza is hardly healthy. Levels of fat, salt and calories are sky-high. OK, so it's less horrible than a cheeseburger, but then so is nearly anything. If you want a really healthy meal, ready in 5 minutes of prep, you can't beat this healthy pizza.

Buy:
- whole-wheat pizza shells
- thick but vegetarian pasta sauce. I like Newman's Own because the profits go to charity and it's not super-high in salt.
- cheese substitute (Daiya is the best) or non-fat mozzarella cheese.
- veggies. Cut them up, nuke them from frozen or pull them out of their pack. Mushrooms and spinach are very healthy. You can slice a zucchini in less than a minute.

Here is the complete procedure:

1. Pull the pasta sauce and whole wheat pizza crust out of the pantry.
2. Set oven to 425 or 450 (whatever the wrapper on the pizza says).
3. Go into the fridge and pull out zucchini and pre-sliced mushrooms and spinach and shredded cheese or cheese sub.
4. Lay the pizza crust on aluminum foil. Put a thin layer of pasta sauce on the crust. Put the remainder in the fridge.
5. Put a relatively thin layer of the cheese (especially if it's real cheese). Now slice the zucchini nice and thin. Lay the slices out so they cover the cheese.
6. Put the mushrooms on the zucchini. Put the spinach on half the mushrooms. Put extra cheese on the rest of the surface of the mushrooms.
7. If you bought fake pepperoni (oh, yum, and no fat or cholesterol), put it on!
8. Did you put the crust on a broiling pan or something? Hope so 'cuz you're going to put the broiling pan in the oven now. That pizza is loaded. Don't drop it.
9. The oven probably isn't at full temperature yet. So add a couple of minutes to the time the wrapper says to bake it for.
10. When the timer goes off, take a look at the crust. Crispy the way you like it?

Recipe 15: Mini-Pizzas

You need: 1 medium to large eggplant, cheese, some mushrooms or spinach, pasta sauce, a protein source and sweet spices.
You need a broiler or an oven that can be set to broil.

Here is the complete procedure:

1. Turn on (heat up) the broiler.
2. Lay a sheet of aluminum foil on the counter.
3. Slice the eggplant thin, but thick enough to hold the mini-pizza ingredients.
4. Lay them down on the foil. Put some pasta sauce on each one. Don't drown it. Less is more here.
5. Put cheese down. You can throw it on willy-nilly if you're in a hurry.
6. Put a mushroom or some spinach on each eggplant.
7. Distribute the protein – chicken substitute, salad shrimp, fake pepperoni, etc.
8. Put the foil on the broiling pan and set it in the broiler.
9. Every broiler has its own procedure. Keep an eye on it the first time to get the timing. Then write it down here so you don't forget._____

Take them out when the pizzas are ready.

Have a nice salad to go with it. If you don't, you (and guests) will grab for carbs. If you're too tired for a salad, toss a parfait together or grab a nice (unsweetened) yogurt for some more protein.

Recipe 16: Baked Macaroni and Cheese

Are you nuts? I can hear you thinking. How could mac-and-cheese be healthy?

It's possible. It's going to take a bit more than 5 minutes of prep time if you haven't pre-cooked the mac. **The macaroni needs to be whole-grain.** No exceptions. Step away from the white pasta and no one will get hurt, especially not you and your cardiovascular system. There are whole-grain elbows, twists and other cool shapes. Go for small shapes for better mixing.

Assuming that you have cooked pasta (hot or cold, it doesn't matter) ready to go, here is the procedure:

1. Get your oven pre-heated to 350.
2. Get one of your glass baking dishes and put a shallow layer of water and olive oil in the bottom.
3. In a bowl, mix pasta, veggies like mushrooms or spinach and cheese. Use Daiya fake cheese or no-fat cheese, shredded.
4. When it is completely mixed and the cheese in particular is well-mixed, layer it in the baking dish.
5. Sprinkle olive oil on top. Just a bit; don't drown it.
6. Put it in the oven and set the timer for 20 minutes.
7. Check it after 20 minutes. You are looking to see that the cheese has melted. Depending on what you use, it could need a bit more time.

There is another way to make mac and cheese that doesn't involve baking. Look under Pastas in Section 2.

101 Healthy Meals

Recipes 17-19: Lasagna

This is another one of those things that can be very fast and very healthy, if you choose your ingredients carefully.

You need: Whole-grain lasagna, or spinach lasagna; Pasta Sauce; Low-fat cheese or cheese substitute; Protein

Recipe 17: Fake Meat Lasagna

1. Heat oven to 350.
2. Olive oil lightly on the bottom of your glass baking dish.
3. Put cooked lasagna into a layer on the bottom.
4. Layer in veggies like spinach along with fake ground round or Mexican-style burger. You can also chop up the fake Italian sausage, chorizo or Polish sausage.
5. Add pasta sauce so that everything is pretty saturated.
6. Add cheese and sweet prices.
7. Put another layer of lasagna on the top.
8. Lightly sprinkle olive oil on top.
9. Put in the oven and check after 20 minutes. It could need as much as 35 depending on the oven and the specific ingredients. You are looking for melted cheese and a browning upper lasagna layer.

Recipe 18: Real Meat

1. Heat oven to 350.
2. Olive oil lightly on the bottom of your glass baking dish.
3. Put cooked lasagna into a layer on the bottom.
4. Layer in veggies like spinach along with chicken or turkey. [Seriously, doesn't Recipe 17 sound even better?]
5. Add pasta sauce so that everything is pretty saturated.
6. Add cheese and sweet spices.
7. Put another layer of lasagna on the top.
8. Lightly sprinkle olive oil on top.
9. Put in the oven and check after 20 minutes. It could need as much as 35 depending on the oven and the specific ingredients. You are looking for melted cheese and a browning upper lasagna layer.

Recipe 19: Seafood Lasagna

See assumptions under Recipe 17.

Here is the complete procedure:

1. Heat oven to 350.
2. Olive oil lightly on the bottom of your glass baking dish.
3. Put cooked lasagna into a layer on the bottom.
4. Layer in veggies like spinach along with salad shrimp, fake crabmeat or leftover baked fish. Scallops don't work as well here.
5. Add pasta sauce so that everything is pretty saturated.
6. Add cheese and sweet prices.
7. Put another layer of lasagna on the top.
8. Lightly sprinkle olive oil on top.
9. Put in the oven and check after 20 minutes. It could need as much as 35 depending on the oven and the specific ingredients. You are looking for melted cheese and a browning upper lasagna layer.

Recipe 20: Leftovers & Frozen Veggies Casserole

Ingredients: frozen veggies, leftover protein or anything frozen except red meat or seafood.

Here's how it goes:
1. Pull out your glass baking dish.
2. Set oven to 450F.
3. Spray or lightly oil the dish.
4. Add a half-inch or so of water to the dish.
5. Toss the frozen veggies in until they fill up most of the dish.
6. Add a drizzle of olive oil to the top.
7. Add sweet spices
8. Lay the leftover protein on top – or the frozen whatever (see notes under ingredients)
9. Add walnuts. [You really need to keep these stocked, right?]
10. Drizzle olive oil on top, wherever it isn't already.
11. Add sweet prices liberally throughout.
12. Stick in the oven for 20 minutes. If the oven wasn't at 450 yet, add a few minutes to the cook time.

Recipe 21: Fish Bake #1

Ingredients: frozen fish and frozen veggies.

What kind of fish: any white fish will do. Tilapia seems to have less carcinogens than most and it has some flavor. Stay away from tuna, swordfish and any other top-predators. They concentrate all the PCBs and other carcinogens from all the predation layers below them. Not good. Predators like us need to eat at close to the start of the food chain as possible.

Salmon has lots of nice Omega-3's. It's a fatty fish, though, so it will need an extra minute of cook time, and less olive oil.

Here's how it goes:

1. Heat oven to 450F.
2. Oil the glass baking dish.
3. The dish: I use the biggest one I have and use 4 fish fillets so I have leftovers and don't have to cook dinner tomorrow. Hooray.
4. Add half-inch or so of water to the dish.
5. Layer the veggies on the bottom. Have at least a cup for every fish fillet you use.
6. Oil lightly on top, and add sweet spices or the onion family (not both, unless you're feeling very daring).
7. Lay the fish across the top. Bake as many as you can in one session.
8. Drizzle more olive oil and sprinkle more spices.
9. Place dish in oven.
10. Set for 20 minutes. Add more if the oven wasn't completely heated.

    Test the fish for flakiness. If it's tough, it needs more cooking. I bake until the fish are brown and crispy at the edges, but that's just me.

Recipe 22: Fish Bake #2

Ingredients: frozen fish and frozen veggies, pasta sauce.

What kind of fish: any white fish will do. Tilapia seems to have less carcinogens than most and it has some flavor. Stay away from tuna, swordfish and any other top-predators. They concentrate all the PCBs and other carcinogens from all the predation layers below them. Not good. Predators like us need to eat at close to the start of the food chain as possible. Don't do this with salmon.

Here's how it goes:

1. Heat oven to 450F.
2. Oil the glass baking dish.
3. The dish: I use the biggest one I have and use 4 fish fillets so I have leftovers and don't have to cook dinner tomorrow. Hooray.
4. Add half-inch or so of water to the dish.
5. Layer the veggies on the bottom. Have at least a cup for every fish fillet you use.
6. Oil lightly on top, and add sweet spices or the sharp onion family (not both, unless you're feeling very daring).
7. Lay the fish across the top. Bake as many as you can in one session.
8. Add the pasta sauce until it goes everywhere. Do this slowly and it will work better. If I have the time, I add some water to the pasta sauce to make it less thick, so it flows better.
9. Sprinkle more spices.
10. Place dish in oven.
11. Set for 20 minutes. Add more if the oven wasn't completely heated.

Test the fish for flakiness. If it's tough, it needs more cooking. I bake until the fish are brown and crispy at the edges, but that's just me.

Recipe 23: Salad Shrimp Bake

Ingredients: frozen salad shrimp (buy it cooked) and frozen veggies.

Here's how it goes:

1. Heat oven to 450F.
2. Oil the glass baking dish.
3. The dish: I use the biggest one I have and use lots of shrimp so I have leftovers and don't have to cook dinner tomorrow.
4. Add half-inch or so of water to the dish.
5. Layer the veggies on the bottom. Have at least a cup for every portion of shrimp you use.
6. Add walnuts.
7. Oil lightly on top, and add sweet spices or the onion family (not both, unless you're feeling very daring).
8. Lay the shrimp across the top. Bake as many as you can in one session.
9. Drizzle more olive oil and sprinkle more spices.
10. Place dish in oven.
11. Set for 20 minutes. Add more if the oven wasn't completely heated.

Don't do this more than twice/week. Shrimp are high in cholesterol.

Recipe 24: Jumbo Shrimp Bake

Ingredients: frozen jumbo shrimp (make sure they're cooked) and frozen veggies. Sometimes I take the crunchy tails off before they cook, but they taste good with them on, too. They won't kill you unless you gulp them down too fast. Eat slower.

Here's how it goes:

1. Heat oven to 450F.
2. Oil the glass baking dish.
3. The dish: I use the biggest one I have and use lots of shrimp so I have leftovers and don't have to cook dinner tomorrow. Hooray.
4. Add half-inch or so of water to the dish.
5. Layer the veggies on the bottom. Have at least a cup for every portion of shrimp you use.
6. Add walnuts.
7. Oil lightly on top, and add sweet spices or the onion family (not both, unless you're feeling very daring).
8. Lay the jumbo shrimp across the top. Bake as many as you can in one session.
9. Add the pasta sauce. Add some water to the sauce so it flows more smoothly if you like or just ladle it in carefully.
10. Drizzle more olive oil and sprinkle more spices.
11. Place dish in oven.
12. Set for 20 minutes. Add more if the oven wasn't completely heated.

This tastes different than the salad shrimp version. They have a heavy dose of cholesterol so stay away from LDLs in the rest of your eating for a day or two.

Recipe 25: Scallops Bake

Ingredients: frozen scallops and frozen veggies.

Here's how it goes:

1. Heat oven to 450F.
2. Oil the glass baking dish.
3. Add half-inch or so of water to the dish.
4. Layer the veggies on the bottom. Have at least a cup for every portion of shrimp you use.
5. Oil lightly on top, and add sweet spices or the onion family (not both, unless you're feeling very daring).
6. Lay the scallops across the top. Bake as many as you can in one session.
7. Drizzle more olive oil and sprinkle more spices.
8. Place dish in oven.
9. Set for **30 minutes**. Add more if the oven wasn't completely heated.

Scallops need more cooking time. Check them. If your fork gets resistance, cook some more. Crispy veggies taste great, but undercooked scallops are a trial.

Recipe 26: Crab and Fake Crab Bake

Ingredients: crab or (cheaper) fake crab meat and frozen veggies. Sometimes I add some real crab to the fake for a different flavor without adding too much extra expense. Fake crab is just a less-expensive fish's flesh, pressed into crab "shape." It's very healthy.

Here's how it goes:

1. Heat oven to 450F.
2. Oil the glass baking dish.
3. The dish: I use the biggest one I have and use lots of protein so I have leftovers and don't have to cook dinner tomorrow. Hooray.
4. Add half-inch or so of water to the dish.
5. Layer the veggies on the bottom. Have at least a cup for every portion of crab you use.
6. Oil lightly on top, and add sweet spices or the onion family (not both, unless you're feeling very daring).
7. Lay the crab across the top. Bake as many as you can in one session.
8. Drizzle more olive oil and sprinkle more spices.
9. Place dish in oven.
10. Set for 20 minutes. Add more if the oven wasn't completely heated.

No testing for flakiness.

Recipe 27: Italian Crab and Fake Crab Bake

Ingredients: crab or (cheaper) fake crab meat (or some of each) and frozen veggies. Pasta sauce.

Here's how it goes:

1. Heat oven to 450F.
2. Oil the glass baking dish.
3. The dish: I use the biggest one I have and use lots of protein so I have leftovers and don't have to cook dinner tomorrow. Hooray.
4. Add half-inch or so of water to the dish.
5. Layer the veggies on the bottom. Have at least a cup for every portion of crab you use.
6. Oil lightly on top, and add sweet spices or the onion family (not both, unless you're feeling very daring).
7. Lay the crab across the top. Bake as many as you can in one session.
8. Drizzle more olive oil and sprinkle more spices.
9. Add pasta sauce, making sure that it goes everywhere.
10. Place dish in oven.
11. Set for 20 minutes. Add more if the oven wasn't completely heated.

See if the sauce looks crusty… taste test. You might need more bake time depending on your oven.

Recipe 28: Italian Sausage Bake

Ingredients: Sausage substitute and frozen veggies. After you detox your taste buds, the real stuff will taste so fatty you'll want to throw up if you eat it.

Here's how it goes:

1. Heat oven to 450F.
2. Oil the glass baking dish.
3. The dish: I use the biggest one I have and use lots of protein so I have leftovers and don't have to cook dinner tomorrow. Hooray.
4. Add half-inch or so of water to the dish.
5. Layer the veggies on the bottom. Have at least a cup for every portion of sausage you use.
6. Oil lightly on top, and add sweet spices or the onion family (not both, unless you're feeling very daring).
7. Lay the sausage across the top. Bake as many as you can in one session.
8. Drizzle more olive oil and sprinkle more spices.
9. Place dish in oven.
10. Set for 25 minutes. Add more if the oven wasn't completely heated.

Recipes 29-30: Polish sausage and Chorizo bakes

Different tastes. Safeway has this stuff and it tastes much fattier (yummy) than it sounds.

Recipe 31: Quesadilla (kay-sa-DEE-ya)(If you're going to eat it, you might as well say it correctly)

Ingredients: whole-wheat or spinach tortilla (tore-TEA-ya), cheese substitute or low-fat mozzarella, shredded veggies, sliced tomato. No added sauces, sour cream or guacamole. [I saw you trying to sneak it in there. Cut that out.] A SMALL amount of mushed up avocado if you must.

Here's how it goes:

1. Turn the broiler on or get ready to nuke.
2. Lay the tortilla down.
3. Lightly cover with the shredded cheese.
4. Layer thinly sliced tomato.
5. Layer thinly sliced zucchini or other veggies (green leafy stuff like kale is great) where the tomato isn't.
6. Sprinkle olive oil on top.
7. Add sweet spices, lightly.

Broil until the cheese bubbles or microwave for 60 seconds.

Slice into small triangles. Add avocado. [Small amount, right?]

Recipe 32: Meat and Rice Casserole

Ingredients: Ground round or Mexican-flavor fake meat [versions are soy, wheat or other textured plant protein with zero cholesterol and fat]; pre-cooked rice; peas and carrots (frozen, not canned); walnuts.

Here's how it goes:

1. Heat oven to 450F.
2. Oil the glass baking dish.
3. The dish: I use the biggest one I have so I have leftovers and don't have to cook dinner tomorrow. Hooray.
4. Mix the veggies and rice together in a bowl, then add the fake ground round.
5. Add walnuts.
6. Put mixture in dish.
7. Oil lightly on top, and add sweet spices or the onion family
8. Place dish in oven.
9. Set for 20 minutes. Add more if the oven wasn't completely heated.

Recipe 33: Meat & Brown Rice Casserole (rice wasn't pre-cooked version)

Ingredients: Ground round or Mexican-flavor fake meat; uncooked brown (minute type) rice; peas and carrots (frozen, not canned).

Warning: this usually doesn't work with wild-grain rice and it may be a bit underdone if it's the non-minute rice…. Experiment.

Here's how it goes:

1. Heat oven to 350F.
2. Oil the glass baking dish.
3. The dish: I use the biggest one I have so I have leftovers and don't have to cook dinner tomorrow. Hooray.
4. Add a three-quarter inch to a half-inch or so of water to the dish.
5. Mix the veggies and rice together in a bowl, then add the fake ground round.
6. Add walnuts.
7. Oil lightly on top, and add sweet spices or the onion family.
8. Put into dish. The rice needs to soak up the water. Be aware that the rice will expand and don't overfill the dish!
9. Place dish in oven.
10. Set for 30-40 minutes. Add more if the oven wasn't completely heated.

Recipe 34: Italian Meat and Rice Casserole

Ingredients: Ground round or Mexican-flavor fake meat; pre-cooked rice; peas and carrots (frozen, not canned). Pasta sauce. Walnuts.

Here's how it goes:

1. Heat oven to 450F.
2. Oil the glass baking dish.
3. The dish: I use the biggest one I have so I have leftovers and don't have to cook dinner tomorrow. Hooray.
4. Add half-inch or so of water to the dish.
5. Mix the veggies and rice together in a bowl, then add the fake ground round.
6. Add walnuts.
7. Add pasta sauce.
8. Lay in glass baking dish.
9. Oil lightly on top, and add sweet spices or the onion family
10. Place dish in oven.
11. Set for 20 minutes. Add more if the oven wasn't completely heated.

Recipe 35: Sauteed Tomatoes and Vegetarian Chicken with Brown Rice (pre-cooked version)

Ingredients: Fresh tomato (1 large beefsteak or 2 small; not the cherry size); vegetarian "chicken"; pre-cooked brown rice.

Here's how it goes:

1. Warm up the rice. You can add a bit of water and nuke it for 60 seconds or stick it in the oven as it preheats – whatever you like.
2. Get your fry pan oiled and heat to medium.
3. Meanwhile, slice the tomatoes as thin as you can without adding human tissue to the food.
4. Saute the tomatoes. Add the vegetarian chicken. Flip them until both sides are nice and crispy.
5. Put the warm rice in a bowl, dump the fry pan contents on top and dig in.
6. Use the pre-heated oven to throw in something to eat tomorrow. [See other baked recipes.)

Recipe 36: Sauteed Tomatoes and Vegetarian Chicken with Brown Rice (uncooked version)

Ingredients: Fresh tomato (1 large beefsteak or 2 small; not the cherry size); vegetarian "chicken"; uncooked minute-style brown rice or a pilaf mix (a bit less healthy, but close enough).

Here's how it goes:

1. Get your fry pan oiled and heat to low.
2. Meanwhile, slice the tomatoes as thin as you can without adding human tissue to the food.
3. Put the rice in the pan and add about a half-inch of water to the pan. Put heat up to medium.
4. If you are the worrywart type, stand there and stir while the rice cooks. Alternately, you can go away for 10 minutes (set the timer).
5. If you only have one fry pan, dump out the cooked rice into a bowl and oil up the pan again. If you have two, aren't you glad you do? You can just oil it up and let the rice burble at Low heat for another couple of minutes.
6. Saute the tomatoes. Add the vegetarian chicken. Flip them until both sides are nice and crispy.
7. Put the warm rice in a bowl, dump the fry pan contents on top and dig in.

Use the heated oven to throw in something to eat tomorrow. [See other baked recipes.)

Recipe 37: Veggie Burrito

Ingredient: whole wheat, spinach or similarly non-white tortilla, can of beans, cheese substitute or low-fat mozzarella, small dollop of spicy Mexican sauce, some leftover brown rice, chopped veggies. 4 doses of Beano for everyone who eats.

What kind of beans?
Red, adzuki, garbanzos… anything but refried. WAY too full of fat and god-knows-what. Stay away. You can mash the beans to make them taste more like refried.

Here's how it goes:

- Open and drain the can of beans. Average can is two portions. Mash the beans with a fork if you like.
- Collect the leftover or pre-cooked brown rice. No more than a half-cup per burrito. Collect the veggies.
- Lay the tortilla down.
- Visualize a small rectangle at the center of the tortilla. You will fill that with fillings.
- Start with the beans. Next to it, place a line of rice.
- On top of the beans, place the veggies and the shredded cheese. Finish with a dollop of sauce.
- Now wrap it. Do the ends. Fold them toward the center. Now start at the edge that is between the ends and closest to you.
- Fold your flap over all the way, and then continue folding the cylinder with the filling until the whole thing is completely folded.
- Eat it. Add a salad, with walnuts.

If you are like most people, you will underfill or overfill the first time. If you overfill, it will fall apart and can't be held. So get a knife and fork and eat like a civilized person. Next time will be better! You didn't give up the first time you tried to walk and fell on your butt. Now you can walk, talk and chew gum at the same time, god help us. So don't give up on this either. Someday you will be able to assemble a burrito and explain to your daughter why Easter is a different day every year, at the same time. [It's the first Sunday after the first full moon after the Spring Equinox. But you knew that.]

Recipe 38: Meaty Burrito

Ingredient: whole wheat, spinach or similarly non-white tortilla, can of beans, cheese substitute or low-fat mozzarella, small dollop of spicy Mexican sauce, Mexican-flavor ground round substitute, chopped veggies. 4 doses of Beano for everyone who eats.

What kind of beans?
Red, adzuki, garbanzos… anything but refried. WAY too full of fat and god-knows-what. Stay away. You can mash the beans to make them taste more like refried.

Here's how it goes:

- Open and drain the can of beans. Average can is two portions. Mash the beans with a fork if you like.
- Collect the leftover or pre-cooked brown rice. No more than a half-cup per burrito. Collect the veggies.
- Lay the tortilla down.
- Visualize a small rectangle at the center of the tortilla. You will fill that with fillings.
- Start with the beans. Next to it, place a dollop of the Mexican ground round.
- On top of the beans, place the veggies and the shredded cheese. Finish with a dollop of sauce.
- Now wrap it. Do the ends. Fold them toward the center. Now start at the edge that is between the ends and closest to you.
- Fold your flap over all the way, and then continue folding the cylinder with the filling until the whole thing is completely folded.
- Eat it. Add a salad, with walnuts.

See notes on previous recipe.

Recipe 39: Eggplant Parmagiana

Ingredients: sliced eggplant, pasta sauce, shredded cheese substitute or low-fat mozzarella, sliced other veggies, original or Mexican-flavor ground round substitute.

Here's how it goes:

- Heat oven to 350F
- Get out a nice big glass baking dish and put a layer of olive oil (light) on the bottom.
- Slice the eggplant as thin as you can without slicing your fingers off. (This dish has no human flesh component.) Slice some other veggies.
- Lay the slices of eggplant down so they entirely fill the pan.
- Add a layer of fake ground round. Sprinkle some olive oil.
- Add a thin layer of pasta sauce.
- Add more eggplant and other sliced veggies.
- Add another layer of "meat" and put pasta sauce on top.
- Put a nice generous amount of cheese substitute on top. [Real cheese has a lot of fat. If it's low-fat real cheese, make it a thin layer.]
- Stick it in the oven and bake for 30 minutes or until the cheese starts looking charred.

    Add a salad, with walnuts.

Recipe 40: Carrots!

It's really hard to get carrots into many of these meals, because they usually involve slicing and most carrots are harder than a granitic boulder. You can get your carrot-fix in the casseroles, but what about the rest of the days?

There is a solution and it tastes great: Carrot juice.

Make sure that it is pure, unadulterated carrot with no admixtures. Carrot by itself tastes great, and you know why. [Pop quiz time! Did you remember all that stuff about umami and glutamate? Sure you did.]

Add carrot juice to any meal and you get an eye-popping amount of vitamins, especially the ones that are plentiful in the yellow/orange/red veggies that the Surgeon General is always nattering on about. Help our beloved country lower its rates of cancer, heart disease, diabetes, obesity and general crankiness by drinking carrot juice every day/

Recipe 41: Asparagus and Fish

This taste-treat is so unique that it deserves its own recipe.

Ingredients: asparagus, preferably organic, for the great taste. White fish, maybe tilapia.

Here's how it goes:

1. Heat oven to 350F
2. Water and some olive oil in the bottom of your glass casserole dish.
3. Lay the fish in the center, with the asparagus around it, nicely laid out.
4. Drizzle more olive oil on top.
5. Add sweet spices. Make sure the asparagus get plenty.
6. Bake for 30 minutes or until the fish is flaky.

Add a salad. This is divine!

Recipe 42: Stuffed Peppers

Ingredients: Several LARGE green/red/orange or yellow peppers. Pasta sauce. Sweet spices. COOKED brown rice or other healthy grain; cooked lentils taste particularly good (get lentil soup and save the stock for another day). Chopped veggies. Optional: russet potatoes (NOT the big brown things!) with parsley and sweet spices. Optional: fake sausages.

Here is the complete procedure:

1. Heat oven to 350.
2. Olive oil in a large glass baking dish.
3. Cut the top 20% off the peppers.
4. In a mixing bowl, mix the rice (or lentils) with olive oil and the chopped veggies. Microwave the sausages for 30 seconds, then chop them up and add to the mixture for some added protein.
5. Stuff the mixture into the open green peppers. Put the tops back on.
6. Place the peppers in the glass baking dish. If there is a lot of extra room – oops, get a smaller dish. If there is a little extra room, chop up the russets and place them around the peppers. Sprinkle them liberally with parsley and sweet spices.
7. Add pasta sauce around the tomatoes if desired. Try it with and without. If you don't have pasta sauce, add about a cup of water to the bottom of the dish, so the food doesn't dry out as it bakes.
8. Pop the dish in the oven and bake for 35 minutes. Test one of the tomatoes with a sharp knife. If it feels soft and cuts easily, it's ready. If not, bake another 5-10 minutes and try again. Change this recipe to the correct total time for your oven.

This will give you an entrée for several days.

Or eat it in a combo: Pair with a spinach salad, some hummus or leftover spaghetti squash.

Section 2

Soups, Stew, Skewers and Pasta

This category includes a great deal of my diet, especially during the cold months, when a hot meal is extra-appreciated. During the dark of winter, our bodies crave carbs, so beware and take proactive steps to ensure that you don't try to live on starches for 3-6 months. 'Taint healthy.

Soup and Stew (Read me before you plunge into the recipes)

There are approximately a half-dozen concepts here that you can create in either a soup or a stew form, depending on whether you want a thinner or thicker dish.

Stew: thicker stock (add protein powder, textured vegetable protein or cooked grain to thicken soup) and it has more contents with less fluid. If you are adding grain, you generally don't have to add much and you don't have to precook if it is pilaf or instant brown rice and you simmer the stew for at least 20 minutes on low or low-medium. If you are adding protein powder, resist the call of your chocoholism and stick to plain or vanilla flavor, unless you have a much stronger stomach than mine.

Soup has more fluid and the stock is more watery. You can put your components together and then simmer on low for 20 minutes or low-medium for 10 minutes without watching it. If you're nearby, stir occasionally to help the components heat equally. If you're in another room, the patient won't die.

For each recipe here, you can start in one of two ways:

- Start with a low-sodium commercial soup like minestrone, vegetable, lentil or split pea (without ham).
- Start with plain stock. This has less sodium and is usually the best way to go. I frequently start with water.

Because we are aiming for Healthy, you need to nix saturated fat. That means no beef, pork, lamb, mutton, venison, bison, ostrich or other land animals. Stick to tasty meat substitutes in your local grocery or (for more variety) health food stores or go with free-range chicken or turkey, or a fish that is low on the food chain. No albacore tuna, ever. Small amounts of non-white tuna. Any amount of tilapia or wild Pacific salmon. Atlantic salmon is *verboten*; none of it is wild. [Farmed salmon has 6 times the PCBs of beef, which is full of PCBs. That's a lot of cancer-promoting stuff to be ingesting.]

Pasta

Whole-grain. No exceptions. It's right next to the white stuff on your grocery shelf. If not on the one you generally shop at, check out other mainstream grocery stores. The health food stores have the most options. Run off and stock up. One recipe is for spaghetti squash, which you can treat just like grain pasta after you get it cooked.

In all these pasta dishes, there will be 1/3 pasta by volume or less. Most of the content will be vegetables and protein. Veggies and whole-grain give you vitamins and fiber, and protein gives you body-building components.

Most pasta dishes have a counterpart in the soups & stews section. That's no accident.

Recipe 43: Seafood Soup/Stew

Read the general instructions at the start of the chapter before plunging in.

Ingredients: choose any of all of the following: fake crab; genuine crab; oysters; scallops; fish leftovers; frozen fish; clams; shrimp [any size]. Sweet spices. Fresh or frozen vegetables.

1. Start with vegetable stock, or a low-salt commercial vegetable soup, or water with spices.
2. Put the burner on Medium.
3. Add a package of microwaved frozen veggies (without a sauce, right?). For this recipe, a collection of different tastes works better than a gazillion sliced carrots. If you are using fresh, focus on organic carrots, broccoli, cauliflower, green beans, onions, asparagus, even chard and bok choy. Chop them small. [This will take more than 5 minutes the first time.]
4. Are you using frozen scallops? If you are using frozen scallops, they are the Problem Children. They frequently need more cook time. Set them to microwave for 3 minutes while you chop vegetables or while the veggies start warming up in their pot.
5. Add the rest of the seafood that is frozen.
6. Add sweet spices. Don't be shy or stingy.
7. Don't cover it.
8. Set the timer for 8 minutes.
9. Come back, and lower the heat to low. This is when you add the seafood that isn't frozen.
10. Set the time for 8 again.
11. Come back, serve and enjoy.

Recipe 44: Split Pea Stew/Soup

Stew: textured vegetable protein from the health food store
Soup: low-salt commercial split pea.

1. Start with a low-salt commercial split-pea soup.
2. Put the burner on Medium.
3. Add a package of microwaved frozen green peas – or slit peas if you can find them. Stay away from canned.
4. If this is going to be a stew, add the textured vegetable protein now.
5. Lower to Low-Medium.
6. Add sweet spices. Don't be shy or stingy.
7. Don't cover it.
8. Follow the directions in the start of the chapter.

This is a nice protein dish. Serve with thick, hearty bread.

Recipe 45: Lentil Soup/Stew

Stew: textured vegetable protein from the health food store
Soup: low-salt commercial split pea.

1. Start with a low-salt commercial lentil soup.
2. Put the burner on Medium.
3. Add a package of canned beans. Red beans work well with lentils.
4. If this is going to be a stew, add the textured vegetable protein or other thickening now. You can chop up veggie hotdogs and veggie sausage and add them now. I don't heat them before adding them.
5. Add sweet spices. Don't be shy or stingy.
6. Don't cover it.
7. Follow the directions in the start of the chapter.

This is a nice protein dish. Serve with thick, hearty bread.

Recipe 46: Three Bean [Five Bean] Stew/Soup

Read the general instructions at the start of the chapter before plunging in.

This works like any other soup or stew.

1. Start with a bunch of different types of low-salt canned beans. Buy the best quality you can afford because this is a major source of protein. Drain the cans and dump the beans into a pot with a can or two of water. [You drain the can because you don't want the salt and preservatives they were stored in.]
2. Simmer with sweet spices on Low. Set the timer for 20 minutes.

    Take plenty of Beano as you eat.

    Munch hearty thick bread with olive oil spread

Recipe 47: Vegetable Stew/Soup

Read the general instructions at the start of the chapter before plunging in. Choose the Dog recipe (#48) if you want a chunky, hearty, "hungry man" version. [Meat is ideologically linked with masculinity in American culture, but fat and cholesterol don't build muscles or health; they are a major source of debility and weakness – hardly "masculine."]

1. Start with commercial vegetable or minestrone low-salt soup or water with spices.
2. Add a package of microwaved frozen veggies. For this recipe, a collection of different tastes works better than a gazillion sliced carrots. If you are using fresh, focus on carrots, broccoli, cauliflower, green beans, onions, asparagus, even chard and bok choy. Chop them small. [This will take more than 5 minutes the first time.]
3. Add a can of extra water for each package of veggies.
4. For stew, add the extras as explained at the start of the chapter.
5. Add sweet spices.
6. Simmer on Low for 15 minutes.

    Munch hearty thick bread with olive oil spread

Recipe 48: Veggie Dog & Sausage Stew/Soup
Read the general instructions at the start of the chapter before plunging in.

This is a fun soup/stew.

1. Set a pot on Low-Medium, with water and sweet spices or a low-salt commercial soup with extra sweet spices.
2. Chop chunks of veggie/tofu hotdogs or veggie sausage into the soup.
3. If stew, add the textured vegetable protein now.
4. Dump the package of frozen veggies in, or add chopped fresh veggies.
5. Set the timer for 20 minutes.
6. An interesting variation is to mix some Grey Poupon into the water while the soup/stew is heating.

   Eat with a spinach salad and walnuts.

Recipe 49: Asparagus and Onion Stew/Soup
Read the general instructions at the start of the chapter before plunging in.

1. Set a pot on Low-Medium, with water and sweet spices or a low-salt commercial vegetable soup with extra sweet spices.
2. Chop chunks of asparagus into the soup. Alternatively, you can leave the asparagus whole, chopping off only the inedible ends. These produce different taste sensations.
3. If stew, add the textured vegetable protein now.
4. Chop onions so that you end up with big circles of onion, in other words, cutting across the widest part of the onion. Place the big circles in the soup.
5. An alternative is to buy pre-chopped onion. You won't get the big circles but it saves time. It's a different taste sensation. If you're allergic to onions, or find that they upset your stomach, leave them out and make this asparagus soup/stew about the sweet spices.
6. Set the timer for 20 minutes.

Asparagus has a really special taste.

Recipe 50: Seafood Pasta (w or w/o Meatballs)

Read the general instructions at the start of the chapter before plunging in.
Ingredients: whole wheat pasta (spirals, elbows, angel hair, it doesn't matter), olive oil, seafood*, vegetarian pasta sauce or Daiya cheese, sweet spices. Optional: veggie meatballs.
* *You want Surimi (fake crabmeat), flake style, salad shrimp (not too often; high in cholesterol), clams or other seafood. Stay away from anything packed in oil, or with a sauce. Just plain protein.*

Decide: vegetarian pasta sauce or cheese sauce? The cheese needs to be Daiya brand non-dairy cheese.

This is the entire procedure:

1. Get a 2 quart pot, fill it half full and set it on HIGH.
2. When the water is boiling, add half a package of whole-wheat pasta and a bit of olive oil.
3. Set timer for 8 minutes and lower heat to Med-High, enough to keep it boiling but not to boil over. Experiment until you know what works for your stove.
4. A) Red sauce option:
   While that it cooking, microwave the pasta sauce and the seafood in a big bowl until it's warm. 1.5 min is enough. Every microwave is different so start with a minute and check it.
4. B) Cheese sauce option: Nuke the seafood for 45 seconds. Put it in a big bowl.
5. Microwave the veggie meatballs. You can combine this with the sauce/seafood if you are going with red sauce. Or you can nuke it on its own if going with cheese sauce. Follow package directions.
6. Check the pasta to make sure it's done – scoop one out and chomp on it. A little al dente is good. Undercooked is bad. Keep cooking and checking. When the pasta is done, use a colander to get rid of the water.
7. Red sauce option: Dump the pasta in with the red sauce. Add spices. You're done!
8. Cheese sauce option: coat the pasta with a thin film of olive oil. The sprays are good for this. Use a mixing spoon to make sure that everything gets coated. Mix about half a package of Daiya mozzarella in. The olive oil makes it stick to the pasta. You now have pasta, seafood and cheese. Add spices. You're done!

This meal has lots of good fiber and carbs, and lots of no-fat protein. What it lacks is veggies. Make it a seafood primavera (see recipe in this section) or have a nice generous spinach salad with tangerine slices and vinegar dressing. [Put the bleu-cheese down.]

Recipe 51: Pasta Primavera
Read the general instructions at the start of the chapter before plunging in.

Ingredients: whole wheat pasta (spirals, elbows, angel hair, it doesn't matter), olive oil, chopped fresh or frozen veggies, Daiya cheese, sweet spices. Make sure that you have twice as much veggies as pasta. If using long strand spaghetti, break the strands in two before you cook them.

This is the entire procedure:

1. Get a 2 quart pot, fill it half full and set it on HIGH.
2. When the water is boiling, add half a package of whole-wheat pasta and a bit of olive oil.
3. Set timer for 8 minutes and lower heat to Med-High, enough to keep it boiling but not to boil over. Experiment until you know what works for your stove.
4. Nuke the veggies for 90 seconds to 2.5 minutes – some veggies need more time. Put it in a big bowl.
5. Check the pasta to make sure it's done – scoop one out and chomp on it. A little al dente is good. Undercooked is bad. Keep cooking and checking. When the pasta is done, use a colander to get rid of the water.
6. Dump the pasta in with the veggies.
7. Coat the pasta with a thin film of olive oil. The sprays are good for this. Use a mixing spoon to make sure that everything gets coated. Mix about half a package of Daiya mozzarella in. The olive oil makes it stick to the pasta.
8. Add sweet spices and mix some more.
9. You don't need to add Parmesan (too much fat, umami, etc.) because you already have cheese flavor. Romano is a nice grated cheese with much less umami and fat.

It makes sense to make a double or triple batch of this and eat it for several days or at least cook up a batch of pasta and use it in two different dishes. A double or triple batch usually needs more cook time.

101 Healthy Meals

Recipe 52: Pasta With Meatballs

Read the general instructions at the start of the chapter before plunging in.

Ingredients: whole wheat pasta; fresh or frozen green beans, baby carrots or succotash; veggie meatballs. [Come on, you thought I was going to let you slip some high-fat, PCB-laden junk in here?] Vegetarian pasta sauce, Daiya brand non-dairy cheese.

This is the entire procedure:

1. Get a 2 quart pot, fill it half full and set it on HIGH.
2. When the water is boiling, add half a package of whole-wheat pasta and a bit of olive oil.
3. Set timer for 8 minutes and lower heat to Med-High, enough to keep it boiling but not to boil over. Experiment until you know what works for your stove.
4. Red sauce option:
   While that it cooking, microwave the pasta sauce and veggies in a big bowl until it's warm. 1.5 min is enough. Every microwave is different so start with a minute and check it.
5. Microwave the veggie meatballs. You can combine this with the sauce. Or you can nuke it on its own. Follow package directions.
6. Check the pasta to make sure it's done – scoop one out and chomp on it. A little al dente is good. Undercooked is bad. Keep cooking and checking. When the pasta is done, use a colander to get rid of the water.
7. Dump the pasta in with the red sauce and veggies. Add spices.
8. Mix about half a package of Daiya mozzarella in.

Recipe 53: Get Skewered!

Read the general instructions at the start of the chapter before plunging in. These are best for times when you have additional chefs or it's not the end of a long, exhausting workday.

Ingredients: disposable bamboo skewers; something to skewer; a bed to put it on.

A skewer dish has two components: what's on the skewer and what's in the bed.
To do this, pick one from column A and one from column B, like what you do for the INS if you don't have a passport.

Skewer options	Bed options
Jumbo shrimp	Greens like spinach with olive oil & vinegar
Scallops [these are notorious slow cookers]	Brown rice or whole grain pilaf
Chunks of flavored tofu [not the white stuff unless you are in training as a martyr]	Whole wheat pasta
Sliced zucchini and other veggies that are not too hard or too soft. Organic baby carrots, yes. Regular carrots, no.	Spaghetti pasta [See Recipe in this book]
Sliced fruits [dessert]	Steamed "solid" veggies

The basic procedure goes like this, for everything but the fruit:

1. Prepare the bed while you are broiling or microwaving the skewer components, so they complete at approximately the same time. Yes, you can do this in 5 minutes of prep if you have the pasta or rice as leftovers.
2. When I am working with seafood and tofu, I usually just microwave them for a few minutes. If the seafood is frozen, you need 3 minutes to unfreeze them, then cook the components another 2 minutes together.
3. When the frozen has been unfrozen, I assemble the skewers and cook/broil them on the skewers.
4. When I am doing veggies, I generally broil until the veggies look singed. Your oven will vary, so I won't suggest a time except to say "not long."
5. Assemble skewers with a seafood, then a veggie, then a seafood, then 2 veggies; repeat. It makes life more colorful and interesting that way.

The procedure for fruit does not involve cooking the poor darlings. Just prepare a nice yogurt dressing for them. They taste great with any bed.

Recipe 54: Grill the Night Away!

Read the general instructions at the start of the chapter before plunging in.

If you're not a grilling aficionado – guilty! – then try it out at a friend's. You might get addicted, especially if you live in a place where the sun comes out a lot, like basically anywhere in the bottom 3/4 of the country.

To avoid saturated fat, you need to say no to red meats.

Grill:

- Tofu (either get the flavored kind or marinade it in low-salt soy sauce – watch the fat content as well as the salt!)
- Fish
- Chicken or turkey without their skins
- Portobello mushroom tops
- Veggie hotdogs
- Veggie burgers
- Veggie sausages

After you grill your protein, pick one of these options:

- Chop it up and mix it in a big salad, with olive oil and fancy vinegar dressing. [I saw you trying to convince your conscience that "Italian" is the same. It's not.]
- Lay the beast down whole on a bed of greens. Remember what color "greens" are – green. Not the color of icebergs.
- Dipped with yogurt sauce, made with plain non-fat yogurt. Go for the high protein, high flavor Greek-style.

One of the greatest joys of life is a grilled veggie hotdog from one of the tasty, high-end companies, slathered with Grey Poupon, and wrapped in some Dave's Sprouted Grain bread. Some people think that hotdogs were invented specifically to give humanity an excuse to eat really good mustard. Just stay away from meat 'dogs. The carcinogens in those things are no joke.

Section 3:

Eating Vegetables, Eating Fruit, Eating Whole Grains & Legumes

Vegetables

In this section, I want to help you with some general veggie cooking ideas, as well as present some veggie entrée ideas.

Which veggies do you need more of:
1. Anything red/orange/yellow. Peppers.
2. Onions and things in the onion family.
3. Tomatoes [yeah, yeah, technically a fruit, but eaten like a veggie. Don't make me come over there and slap you, smart aleck.]
4. Carrots or carrot juice
5. Broccoli, cauliflower and other things that you need to take with Beano.
6. Asparagus. Drizzled with olive oil and sweet spices and well-cooked, this is to die for.
7. Green beans

There are hundreds more, but if you make sure that every dinner and most lunches have good amounts of these, you will improve your health enormously. One limp iceberg lettuce leaf on a sandwich, by the way, is not a vegetable portion to anyone except former President(s) Bush. Stock up on frozen veggies, without sauces, and add them to every meal except oatmeal.

Vegetables not only have lots of vitamins, they also have fiber. The Breakfast section has some breakfast fiber options and the rest of the sections have whole-grain fiber. You can also help your digestion and your heart with daily doses of **psyllium**, which comes in nice ground versions that you can add to smoothies, sprinkle into casseroles and just gulp down with drinks.

Which don't include carbonated drinks or alcohol, right? Carbonated drinks have high acid content, which depletes your body of calcium and weakens your bones, and too much phosphorus, ditto. This is SERIOUS! Step away from the Diet Coke unless you keep it open and let it go "flat" for a good long time. Drink water flavored with Stevia in some of the amazing flavors it comes in. They sell it in ordinary grocery stores, although for the widest selection of flavors you would go to a health food store. Refill water bottles with various flavors.

Alcohol in very small quantities like *1-2 glasses a week* has no ill effects and you can cut back on other food to make up for the empty calories. If you've been drinking more than that, we need to talk. Forget about the red wine preventing heart disease clap-trap. Sure there is a small positive effect because booze relaxes you and red wine has some good flavonoids. But you get a much larger antioxidant "bang" from even moderate exercise, without the calories, and you can relax much better and faster, without getting stupid along with relaxed, through Reiki or meditation. Go beer-tasting or wine-tasting for unique flavors once/month and leave it alone the rest of the time. Your arteries, your waistline, your family, your finances and everyone else on the road will thank you. The wine producers can find something else to grow. [No, not THAT stuff…..]

Here are some easy ways to add veggies:

- add veggies to soup or stew (See Soup and Stew sections). Even if you don't think you like soup or stew, give this a look.
- add veggies to a baked dish (see Baked section)
- add veggies to something sautéed (See Breakfast; see Stir Frys)

Some easy ways to prepare veggie sides or mains:
- Slice them, drizzle olive oil and broil, grill or bake them.
- Slice them and nuke them
- Slice them and boil them, if you intend mashing them. You don't need to slice them if they are relatively small.

Before we leave veggies I have to say something about avocados, this year's "wonder food." There is some value in avocado for healthy fats if you eat it in small quantities, very sparingly. All the touted health benefits are available elsewhere, for a lot less calories. Before the California avocado growers pulled together the $$ for an ad campaign, avocados were pig feed. They managed to turn them into an upscale haute-cuisine item and now the healthiest thing on two legs. The power of advertising dollars can elect presidents and turn pig chow into health food. Caveat emptor.

Watch out for "green" drinks. They may tout their veggies but if you look at the contents, you will almost always find more fruit. Fruit is full of sugar, so the resulting drink tastes "good" to your sugar-addicted brain. [See the section on Fruit.]

And stop buying "iceberg" lettuce. When you were a wee small child, you learned your alphabet including *L Is For Lettuce*. You colored it green. It's not supposed to be the color of icebergs. Buy it green. Get swiss chard, green chard, and other greens. The darker the color, the more nutrition, as a general rule.

Recipe 55: Veggies and Seafood

Microwave some mixed veggies from frozen (stick with plain veggies without sauces), microwave or otherwise heat some leftover fish, drizzle olive oil and sweet spices, maybe chop in some scallions. This is great!

Recipe 56: Fish and Rice

Put a ½ inch of water in your baking dish, add minute brown rice and peas/carrots, then put frozen fish on top. Bake a 350F for 60 minutes. Depending on the rice, it might be done earlier or later. Once you figure out the right number, this is the easiest prepare-ahead meal on the planet. Cook it the day before and eat it warmed-up the next day. Or fix this on the weekend, when you can cook for 60 minutes and you're not sitting around starving at the end of a long work day. [You'll stop for junk food on the way home; you know you will!]

Recipe 57: Spaghetti Squash and Leftover Protein

Another super-easy one. Bake the squash on the weekend, then use it as the bed for several meals, with different proteins on top. Sprinkle with olive oil and add sweet herbs or romano cheese along with the protein. Nuts are a protein, by the way.

Recipe 58: Baked or Grilled Sweet Potatoes (or Yams)

Sweet potatoes have some excellent nutrition packed in them. However, drowning them in sauce or gravy is a good way to take that nutrition and flush it down the drain; you'll have so much fat there, you'd be better off staying away from them entirely.

And that's what I did for a decade. Then I started experimenting.

- Slice the sweet potatoes medium-thick.
- Take a glass baking dish or a grilling sheet with aluminum foil and lay the veggies out so that all the surfaces are visible.
- Drizzle nicely with olive oil and sprinkle with a sweet spice like marjoram.
- Bake at 350 for 50-60 minutes. When I'm in a hurry, I do 400 for 30 minutes. Tastes a bit better with a longer slow-bake.

If you have a grill or broiler, drizzle them with the oil and spice and grill/broil until they are cooked all the way through and/or crispy. This is divine!

Recipe 59: Mashed Sweet Potatoes/Yams

You can boil them or bake them and then mash them. Just don't put gravy or sauce on them! Some olive oil based butter substitute is OK. I throw sautéed chicken sub or veggie sausages on top and no one ever misses the sauce!

101 Healthy Meals

Recipe 60: Crispy Greens

If you don't have a blood pressure problem and can salt your food occasionally, this is a nice option, similar in concept to the sliced yams. If you do have a blood pressure problem, just skip the salt. Tastes great either way!

  a. Start with some chard or similar greens.
  b. Spray it with olive oil. [Yes, there are sprays. They are great for salads.]
  c. Sprinkle with salt and pepper or sweet spices.
  d. Now lay the greens on a sheet of aluminum foil and broil them for a few minutes until they are crunchy.

Recipes 61-64: Portobello Mushrooms

These ginormous mushrooms, if sliced to give the largest possible flat surface, can pretend to be steak in your favorite meat recipes.

- Recipe 61: Grilled
  You can drizzle them with olive oil and grill them.

- You can make them a platform for mini-pizzas (see the recipe in this book).

- Recipe 62: Porto Parmigiana
  Use them instead of eggplant in this book's parmagiana recipe.

- Recipe 63: Portobello Platter
  You can grill other veggies – like onions! – and place them on the grilled mushrooms, using the mushies like a platter.

- Recipe 64: Orange Beef
  You can grill them and then use a SMALL amount of orange or soy or other fancy sauce to make them taste like your favorite Chinese restaurant meat indulgence. I once had an Orange Beef at a vegetarian restaurant in Mountain View CA that made me want to propose to the chef, just to ensure I could eat that once a week for the rest of my life. [He was married. Darn.]

Grains

Americans, and modern people in general, eat way too much grain. We need more veggies, more lean protein, more legumes (beans, peas), more whole fruit (not juice) and more green leafy stuff. But that doesn't make all grains evil.

Our ancestors started domesticating grains in various places at various times, in North, Central and South America, North and South China, Southeast Asia, the Sahel and Mesopotamia. They did this because the ancient wild grains were high in protein. [There is a theory that grain domestication was the by-product of an accident that led to beer production; there's some archaeological evidence that supports it. See the hilarious How Beer Saved the World on NetFlix.]

So eating whole-grains, especially heritage (uncommon today; common in earlier times) grains, is a valuable and important part of getting protein and fiber into your diet. The importance of fiber could not be over-estimated. Inadequate amounts of fiber are implicated in every form of cancer – not just colon cancer – as well as strokes, cardiovascular disease and diabetes, all the preventable and common killers of our age. We simply have to get more fiber into our bodies every day, to keep our digestion working the way it needs to, and to move potential carcinogens out of our bodies as quickly as possible. Get used to the whole-grain taste. When your body gets used to psyllium and whole grains, and never, ever a grain that isn't whole-grain, your weight and your LDL cholesterol figures will decline. When you first start using whole grains exclusively, your body will respond with some bloat/gas, and intestinal changes. Just give your body time and take some anti-bloat over-the-counter stuff; it will adjust to "healthy" and be happy!

Explore **oats, quinoa, barley, millet, sprouted grain (grains not turned into flour, so you have more nutrition), teff** and other interesting things you will find in ethnic and health stores. Google "heritage grains." Go to farmer's markets. Explore different types of whole-grain oatmeal. Find alternatives to white rice. There are instant and easy-cook brown rice options. Some restaurants have brown rice options. If not, don't eat at the restaurant more than once/week, at most.

If you don't have time for all of this, pick just one grain to explore every month. Make it an adventure, instead of a chore, and involve the whole family.

Sorry, beer doesn't qualify as a whole-grain side-dish, even if it saved the world....

Legumes

Beans are an excellent source of plant protein, fiber and good carbs. Everyone knows about tofu, a soybean product. Try the spiced and marinade versions now available, and try tempeh. Tempeh is a fermented form of tofu and packs more protein wallop than other forms.

Recipe 65: Tempeh Stir Fry
Slice it and stir-fry with veggies. Put on a bed of greens or brown rice.

Recipe 66: Tempeh Bake
Bake it like chicken or beef in any of the Section 1 recipes.

Recipe 67: Tempeh Salad
Heat it and toss it into salads.

Recipe 68: Tempeh & Veggie Salad
Put it on pizza.

Recipe 69: Tempeh Soup
Drop it into soups.

Pick any recipe in Sections 1-2 in particular, and substitute beans for the fake chicken, and see how many more recipes are actually available to you!

Experiment with all the other kinds of beans as well. Three-bean soup is terrific, but you can add beans to any vegetable soup to make it a protein-rich meal. Add seafood and beans and you get a low-fat dose of protein that no meat can touch for nutritional quality. Black beans, garbanzos (chickpeas), red beans, white beans, navy beans, split peas – the options for legume protein are amazing.

They taste pretty darn good, too! Stock up on Beano if you're prone to flatulence.

Recipe 70: Garbanzo & Cucumber Salad

Ingredients: garbanzos; finely chopped cucumbers (skins on); vinegar.

Splurge on a fancy-tasting vinegar for this one. Be generous with the vinegar. Let it sit and soak for 15 minutes, then drain the vinegar and dig in. Sprinkle some parsley and rosemary.

Fruit

Pardon my lack of enthusiasm. Berries, cantelope and grapefruit are among the best foods on the planet. Many of the recipes include them. You should find ways to add them to every dessert or snack you make. They are packed with vitamins and they give you a nice burst of plant sugar to help make them popular.

Did you hear what I said? Snacks. Dessert.

When you are told "fruits and vegetables," what you hear is "fruits." And you proceed to chow down on fruit – especially the high sugar stuff like bananas – and wonder why your doctor, your health coach and your spouse (or anyone else who gives a damn about your vitality and doesn't want to attend your funeral for at least a hundred years) isn't falling over themselves to congratulate you.

The answer is simple, dear. You are focusing on the dessert. You are going for the sugar. How nice for your sugar addiction. It's not making a major dent in your longevity, nor can it. If you want barley, you have to plant barley, not thistles. If you want to see The Grim Reaper fold up his sickle and find easier prey, you need to eat the right fruits – bananas only on Sunday, honey – and you need to focus on veggies. Get your sugar cravings tamed. Fruit is dessert, and not even Louis XIV lived on dessert. You can't either.

Let's be clear about what fresh fruit isn't:

- Yogurt with "fruit" on the bottom. I swear my husband actually tried this one on me. So forget it. You took a healthy food – plain yogurt and you destroyed it with a ton of sugary syrup. Siggi's Icelandic skyr is the only yogurt I eat with fruit, but I call it dessert, not a fruit portion.

- "Fruit-flavored" anything. It's sugar. Put it down.

- Apple or anything else pie. You're kidding me, right? Your aunt can tout her "low sugar" apple pie until she's blue in the face, but 2+2 always equals 4, in this universe at least. This ain't fruit, it's a sugar-dripping, heart-clogging menace. Do it once a year at Thanksgiving (a SMALL slice) and tell people you have an apple pie allergy the rest of the year.

Fresh fruit needs to be pulpy or a berry. You need to taste the fiber in the food. It needs to be pure, unadulterated apple or pear or whatever. Keep the skin on, wash it thoroughly, even the organic, and eat the whole thing. Well, OK, you don't have to eat the cantaloupe rind. Citrus fruit is great. (I said fruit, not juice, which is full of sugar; if you drink juice, make it full of pulp and only drink a bit).

Recipe 71: Fruit & Cucumber Yogurt Salad

Ingredients: fresh fruit [berries, small-chopped melon]; plain nonfat yogurt; chopped cucumber

Instead of the tart vinegar flavor, see how the Cukes taste mixed with fresh fruit and yogurt

Section 4:

Breakfast

Yes, You DO Want to Eat Breakfast

The root cause of many people's problems with nutrition and weight is really a problem with breakfast. We either don't eat it at all or we eat the wrong things.

If you are trying to lose fat:
You MUST eat breakfast. I don't care how small it is, you must. Eating signals your body that the day has begun. It kicks your metabolism into drive. You start to rev. You start to burn more calories every hour, just sitting there; your basal body temperature rises and so does your basal metabolic rate. You will burn more calories through the day, and eat less in the evening by eating breakfast.

Some people tell me that they get nauseous if they eat before noon, and I believe them. Then I tell them that the nausea is an subconscious habit. You never planned to learn it, but you did and you can unlearn it. [It may take time, but anything learned can be unlearned, I promise you. Your brain is composed of neural pathways, not concrete. Now your brother-in-law, that's a different story…...]

Start with something easy and light. If you can drink, you can drink a protein smoothie. Start with small amounts and gradually build up. Close your eyes and tell your subconscious that it wants this good food and tell your stomach to be calm, calm, calm. Eat some flatbread crackers, dude. Small amounts of low-fat food. You can do it, girlfriend. You learned it and you can learn something new. No healthy person gets physiologically nauseous when eating good food. This is mentally-driven, not physical. Trust me.

And not just any breakfast.

If you are trying to improve your health:
You have to give yourself **protein first thing in the morning**. Not a sugary treat. No donuts, ever. You'll have better luck overthrowing the law of gravity than you will this one. Protein and whole-grains, full stop. Bagels are better than donuts, but they are still a sugary treat (a simple carb). Step away from Panera (at breakfast) and no one will get hurt.

If you think your life will be over if you spend 5 minutes getting a really good, protein breakfast, give me a call. You deserve a free 5 minute Reiki session while you get a grip on reality.

Question: What about breakfast bars?
Stay away from them. Too much fat, including saturated fat, too much sugar, too much junk, no matter how "healthy" they sound. Don't have time for a real breakfast? It takes less than 2 minutes to make a healthy smoothie and toss it into a carry-container.

You don't have two minutes? Really? With the greatest respect – puh-LEESE. Cut the drama. Take a deep breath. You are telling yourself one of two stories.

Here is option 1: The story you're telling yourself is designed to convince you that you are important. Very important. Important people in this culture are people who rush around, busy, busy, busy, right? Guess what? News Flash: You ARE important. You don't need to rush around. You don't need to put on the Busy act. I knew you were important on the day that you were born. You don't have to impress me. Settle in to your body and listen without the constant yammer-yammer of "I'm so busy. I'm so important." For a full minute. That's right …. That's the sound of your body saying it's not impressed either. You and your body: the ultimate team. It needs breakfast. You need to have respect for yourself and stop letting fear (and maybe exhaustion as well) run your life. Get a sitter and take a nap. The next time you see someone posturing around, being "busy," just smile. See through the posturing. Have another sip of un-carbonated, flavored water or the remains of your breakfast smoothie and wait for the dramatics to be over. It will be eventually. Meanwhile, the protein will be feeding your neurons what they need to do brilliant work today.

Here is option 2: Stop using the kids as an excuse. Those kids need you to live long and prosper and they need to learn how to clean the toilet and fold laundry. Uh-huh, they do. Stop over-functioning for kids who at their ages were contributing materially to the household subsistence a hundred years ago [so the helplessness is learned] and you'll have 2 minutes to give yourself health.

Here endeth the sermon.

All of the breakfasts here will give your body what it needs for maximum calorie burn, maximum energy and maximum nutrition.

Recipe 72: Scrambled Eggs with Veggies, Sausage and Bacon

You didn't think I meant real sausage and bacon did you? For a healthy meal? Ye, gads. Turkey versions abound. So do really good-tasting substitutes, especially the Morning Star brand. All my omnivore friends love it.

Ingredients:

- 2-3 egg whites or egg substitute. [Or one egg and the rest whites. Whole eggs have a heap of cholesterol and saturated fat.] Egg substitute is egg white with some yellow food coloring and some eggy flavor – a very healthy food.
- Milk, non-fat or non-cow (optional).
- Fine chopped veggies or pico de gallo.
- Fake sausage or bacon, Morningstar brand preferably.
- Spices.
- Daiya brand or your favorite cheese substitute. Or non-fat mozzarella.

Here's the entire procedure:

1. Beat the eggs in a bowl with the milk, if you use milk. The reason for milk is to make a creamier scramble. It's not necessary. If you don't use milk, and you don't use real eggs, no beating is necessary. Beating mixes the yolk, which is the sole source of the cholesterol and other concerns, and the white, just protein, together.
2. Oil a flying pan, let it heat.
3. While it's heating (you have 30 seconds, so don't dawdle): put the sausage or bacon or both in a bowl. Set microwave for 1 minute. Go back to the stove and add veggies to the pan.
4. Saute the veggies for 1 minute, turning them with a spatula to achieve even heating.
5. Chop up the "meat" that is finished from the microwave.
6. Add to the pan.
7. Now add the eggs. Add spices. Use the spatula to keep moving the cooked egg to the side and allow more egg to cook, until everything looks kind of like cottage cheese or is browned.
8. Add some Daiya cheese substitute to the top. Cook another 45 seconds or so.

Put it on a plate and dig in. Get some sprouted bread and olive-oil-based (or Benecol) butter substitute to spread on it.

Recipe 73 : Veggie Omelet with Meat Substitute, Simple Version

Ingredients:

- 2-3 egg whites or egg substitute. [Or one egg and the rest whites. Whole eggs have a heap of cholesterol and saturated fat.] Egg substitute is egg white with some yellow food coloring and some eggy flavor – a very healthy food.
- Milk, non-fat or non-cow (optional).
- Fine chopped veggies or pico de gallo.
- Fake sausage or bacon, Morningstar brand preferably.
- Spices.

Here's the entire procedure:

1. Beat the eggs in a bowl with the milk, if you use milk. The reason for milk is to make a creamier scramble. Beating mixes the yolk, which is the sole source of the cholesterol and other concerns, and the white, just protein, together.
2. Oil a flying pan, let it heat.
3. While it's heating (you have 30 seconds, so don't dawdle): put the sausage or bacon or both in a bowl. Set microwave for 1 minute. Go back to the stove and add veggies to the pan.
4. Saute the veggies for 1 minute, turning them with a spatula to achieve even heating.
5. Chop up the "meat" that is finished from the microwave.
6. Add to the pan.
7. Here's the difference: heat up another pan, with olive oil. Add the eggs. Add spices. Use low-medium heat. Tilt the pan left or right to make sure that everything is heating uniformly. When the bottom seems to be firm – use the spatula to lift the egg-mass and look – then, using a big spatula, flip the "pancake" over onto its other side.
8. Add the contents of the other skillet (the veggies, etc.) onto half of the omelet, add the cheese and then use the spatula to fold the other half over on top.
9. Cook for another 45 seconds and serve.

Does this sound like brain-surgery? Once you get good at it, it's – still a pain in the neck compared to scrambled eggs. If you mess it up, pretend that what you produced is what you planned. Never tell anyone what dinner will be ahead of time!

A simpler procedure: *instead of having a warming skillet, you can just microwave the veggies and fake meat with some water for a minute, then chop up the meat substitute and microwave for another 30 seconds.*

Recipe 74 : Veggie Omelet with Meat Substitute and Whole-Wheat Pancakes
[Courtesy of Rick Baird, breakfast chef extraordinary]

This one will take more than 5 minutes if you're doing it all yourself, so if you want to be adventurous on the weekend, plunge! You will definitely enjoy the results.

Ingredients: small russet potatoes; sliced veggies or greens; fake sausage; cheese (non-fat) or cheese substitute like Daiya brand; onion-garlic family of spices; 3 egg whites or egg sub; optional: fake bacon strips.

Here is the entire procedure: [The chef reminds you that timing is important and so it may not come out right the first time. Excelsior!]
1. Dice the russets.
2. Prep your skillet on medium-low with olive oil.
3. While the potatoes are sautéing, microwave the sausages for 30 seconds, then chop them up.
4. Put the sausage bits into a bowl with the chopped-up or shredded-small greens and veggies.
5. Add the veggie-sausage mix to the skillet potatoes and add more oil to the skillet.
6. Add the spices generously.
7. Add the eggs.
8. When the eggs are almost done, add the cheese. If you add cheese too early, it will carmelize.
9. Optional: make some fake bacon in a 2nd pan while you are on step #5.

Get a 2nd chef in the kitchen to do the following while you are working on 1-9:

10. Mix up whole-grain pancake batter, to which you add protein powder (about ¼ as much as the batter.
11. Follow the cooking directions on the package, substituting non-fat versions for whatever the recipe calls for.
12. Add walnuts, blueberries, strawberries or – only one, mind you – a banana.

When the pancakes are done, slather them with olive-oil based butter substitute. Put that syrup down! Well, OK, on your birthday, Christmas and Bolivian Independence Day you can have some low-sugar syrup, just not too much…. Promise me. Thick yogurt, like the Greek or Icelandic styles (skyr) works well too.

Recipe 75: Breakfast Eggs on Toast

Most people eat toast on the side. However, turning your scrambled eggs into an open-faced sandwich gives a different taste treat.

Ingredients:

- 2-3 egg whites or egg substitute. [Or one egg and the rest whites. Whole eggs have a heap of cholesterol and saturated fat. Limit them.] Egg substitute is egg white with some yolk flavor added – a very healthy food.
- Milk, non-fat or non-cow (optional).
- Finely-chopped veggies.
- Spices.
- 2 slices of whole-grain or sprouted bread

Here's the entire procedure:

1. Oil a flying pan, let it heat.
2. Saute the veggies for 1 minute, turning them with a spatula to achieve even heating or microwave them. Saute gives a better taste but "nuking" works if you are super-rushed.
3. Now add the eggs. Use the spatula to keep moving the cooked egg to the side and allow more egg to cook, until everything looks kind of like cottage cheese. Add spices.
4. While the eggs are cooking, pop your bread in the toaster. The better quality bread tastes better untoasted. If you elect to untoast, lay the two slices next to each other on the plate.
5. (Optional) add some Daiya cheese substitute to the top of the eggs. Cook another 15 seconds or so.
6. Dump the eggs on to your bread. Cover all the surface.

Dig in!

Recipe 76: Huevos Rancheros (unauthentic quick style)

This is a wonderful egg dish that, if you want to experience the real thing, has to be served at a good Mexican restaurant or from someone who actually knows how to cook. However, if you want to get sort-of there and you only want to spend your statutory five minutes doing it, this will work!

Ingredients: 3 egg whites or substitutes (or one whole egg and two subs); half a SMALL avocado; salsa or pico de gallo (buy it at any grocery store), small portion; whole-wheat or corn tortilla, full size (or two corn tortillas); hot sauce (optional); milk (optional).

Here is the entire procedure:

1. Beat the eggs in a bowl with the milk, if you use milk. The reason for milk is to make a creamier scramble. It's not necessary. If you don't use milk, and you don't use real eggs, no beating is necessary.
2. Oil a flying pan, let it heat to Low/Medium.
3. Now add the eggs. Use the spatula to keep moving the cooked egg to the side and allow more egg to cook, until everything looks kind of like cottage cheese. Add spices.
4. (Optional) add some Daiya cheese substitute to the top. Cook another 15 seconds or so.
5. While #3 is happening, warm the tortilla. You can microwave it for 15 seconds or stick it in the oven for a few minutes, if you are baking something or have a small baker/broiler. Warm the salsa/pico for just 10 seconds.
6. Place the tortilla(s) on a plate.
7. Smear the crushed avocado over the tortilla.
8. Now add the eggs.
9. Put the salsa or pico over the eggs. Add hot sauce if desired.
10. DON'T add any guacamole or sour cream. I saw you trying to sneak it. Non-fat and low-cal is nonsense when it comes to the entirely meretricious. [Lovely word; look it up and use liberally this week.] Sour cream has no reason to exist in any form. Put it in the trash. Go on. You know you weren't supposed to buy it. Tsk, tsk and pshaw!

It's really yummy just as it is, without being smothered in all that fat and sugar. Eat is slowly and savor all the spices. If you are early into your de-tox from the high-fat, you may be missing a lot. When your taste buds have awakened, this is divine!

Just so you know: you can do this with **a fried egg** instead of a scramble, but that requires you to use whole eggs – way too much cholesterol if you use more than one. So stick to just one if you go fried, and fry it in olive oil.

Recipe 77: French Toast

This sounds decadent and only really works as a healthy meal if you have whole-grain, sprouted or otherwise fiber-filled bread. If you don't, then it's sugar-filled and generally horrible for you.

Ingredients: 2 slices of whole-grain, sprouted or otherwise fiber-filled bread; one egg white, egg substitute or beat-up whole egg; cinnamon; olive-oil based butter substitute or plain yogurt; sliced strawberries or other smaller berries. No syrup. [Not even if it's low-sugar and blessed by the Pope AND the Archbishop of Canterbury, sorry.]

Here's the complete procedure:

1. Mix your egg or your egg white in a flat, wide bowl – something big enough that your bread can eventually lie semi-flat.
2. Warm up your skillet with olive oil on medium heat.
3. Dunk a slice of bread in the egg so that both sides are completely covered.
4. Drop it into the pan, on the extreme left.
5. Do the same for the second slice of bread and put it on the right.
6. Press down with your wide spatula and hear the egg coating sizzle as it cooks.
7. Flip it over on to its second side.
8. If you have extra egg, drop it into the skillet, anywhere the bread isn't. Let it cook through.
9. Put cinnamon on the bread. Smell how wonderful it smells.
10. When both sides are browned, put them on your plate.
11. Slather with a generous layer of plain non-fat yogurt. Dollop more cinnamon. Now add the sliced fruit to the top.

Get a sharp knife and a fork and dig in. Boy, am I hungry just thinking about this!

Recipe 78: Really Healthy Cereal Meals

Version 1: Oatmeal

Make sure that it is ordinary healthy oatmeal, without added flavor or sweeteners. You can add stevia for sweetness without the calories. Stevia doesn't prompt an insulin rush like other sugars. Steel-cut, genuine Scottish or Irish are terms you may see. Ignore that. Read the ingredients. Act like a Customs and Border Protection agent when you are reading labels: trust nothing. [A very grumpy Canadian agent, after grilling me about my exact goals in visiting his country [take pictures of the mountains] and whether I was visiting friends or having a job interview [on a Saturday?] or bringing gifts, asking for an hour-by-hour itinerary, and asking whether I had over $10,000 in US or Canadian currency on me [not even $10,000 in Monopoly money, darlin'], actually asked me whose car I was driving. Uh, mine – hard to imagine, huh? Do I look like a major international car thief? Now that's grumpy.]

Mix with yogurt, cottage cheese or other non-fat, non-sugar dairy protein for an added protein hit, and some fun tastes.

Add berries or other sliced fruit for more vitamins, anti-oxidants and fiber.

Version 2: Yogurt and Cereal

Ingredients: Healthy whole-grain, low sugar cereal; plain yogurt; fruit; cinnamon.

Here's how it goes:

1. Fill your bowl about ¾ full of cereal.
2. Lay a layer of berries or other fruit (sliced mango, yum!) on top.
3. Lay plain yogurt on top.
4. Sprinkle cinnamon liberally.
5. Mix it all up with your spoon.

Version 3: Teff Breakfast [Thank you to my dear sister Aster for introducing me to teff.] Teff is an East African grain that you can find in most health food stores. Versions I've seen need to be heated in a saucepan but as it gets more popular someone is going to develop a microwave version. You add healthy sweetener – guava, honey, stevia. I usually add walnuts because I add walnuts to everything. [Yes, including ice cream. That adds a patina of virtue to an otherwise unfortunate menu choice. And it tastes great.] Teff has a very nutty flavor, sort of like turbocharged oatmeal.

Recipe 79: Sauteed Or Microwaved Protein With Russet Potatoes

Ingredients: thinly sliced or chopped small russet potatoes; chicken substitute in strips; sliced peppers, spinach and zucchini (or other veggies). Yogurt or sweet spices.

Here is the complete procedure:
1. Chop the veggies and the potatoes.
2. Warm up the skillet with olive oil. Start with medium heat.
3. Saute for about 1.5 minutes on medium high, or until they are browning. You want the veggies to lose some crunch and be easier to eat. You will use the sweet spices OR the yogurt, but not both. If you choose spices, add them now so they have time to cook in.
4. Microwave the chicken substitute for 1.5 minutes while you are sautéing.
5. Dump the veggies on a plate, dump the chicken on top.
6. If you didn't use spices while cooking, add a generous portion of plain non-fat yogurt on top (like a sauce), with cinnamon on top.

Russets have more nutrition and less starch than the big brown things, so you can use them in moderation.

Recipe 80 : Smoothies, the Higher-Cal Version (if you just can't cope with a real meal)

When I have to prep for a busy day and run out the door much earlier than my owl-body thinks it should have to, I rely on a smoothie.

If you primarily want health and nutrition, this is the higher-calorie version:

1. Get out the blender.
2. Add soy/nut milk, water and a container of yogurt (small, or the equivalent from a larger container) to the blender.
3. Add cinnamon and cardamom.
4. Add 2-3 scoops of protein powder
5. Add more water or milk/substitute to desired amount.
6. Add berries or other fruit. Watch out for bananas, which have a lot of simple sugar. Half of one is OK, but no more unless an MD who specialized in nutrition and checks with me first says it's OK.
7. Puree. Pour. Enjoy.

What kind of protein powder?
Read the labels very carefully. Look for whey protein; it's the best source. Get the brand with the lowest sugar content. Yeah, I know, you want the banana split or cherries jubilee or Dutch chocolate flavor. I know, bro; I feel your pain. Get out some paints and paint out your grief at not being able to eat sugary treats all day long like you did when you were a kid. Grieve that lost vision of life. Then pull up your socks and eat what's healthy. Get your Reward center focused on other stuff that feels good. The dog has some ideas; so does your spouse.

Recipe 81 : Smoothies, the lowest-cal version

To get all the good taste, with a less-thick consistency and a whole lot less calories:

- Ditch the yogurt or only use half as much
- No milk; water only.
- Use a bit more protein powder.
- Use more cinnamon. Add Vanilla extract. You want your senses so overwhelmed with good tastes that it doesn't notice that you have less actual food.... It works.

Recipe 82 : Breakfast Parfait

Ingredients: about a cup (a small amount) of whole grain, low-sugar cereal; sliced berries or small berries like blueberries (they can be fresh or frozen); plain yogurt; cinnamon.

Here's how it goes:

1. Grab a tallish, cylindrical cup. A coffee mug will do in a pinch, but taller and thinner works better.
2. Layer the cereal thinly but cover the entire bottom for at least ¼ inch.
3. Now add the berries in another equivalent layer.
4. Add the yogurt.
5. Sprinkle cinnamon on the yogurt. Cardamom works well too.
6. Add additional layers of berries, cereal or yogurt to fill the glass.
7. Sprinkle psyllium, wheat germ or other fiber-adders to the mix, with the cereal or the yogurt.

This has protein from the yogurt and good fiber from the cereal, plus more protein, and some good stuff from the berries. A different version is in the Dessert section!

Plunge your spoon in so you get some of at least two tastes (yogurt and berries or berries and cereal, etc.) in each spoonful. Two or more different things tastes "better" than just one. That's why manufacturers (I use the term deliberately) put salt and sugar into everything, including bread. It makes it taste "better" to your brain even when you don't actually need both. But you can train that Reward Center to click in with the good stuff if you give it time, and stop sneaking the old junk. [I saw that. Cut it out.]

Section 5:

Healthy Desserts

I'll tell you a secret: dessert can be healthy, if you take the time to retrain your taste buds to "real food" and not "super-sugar." It's also essential to remember that dessert is a sugar-treat, not a reward for good behavior, a comfort when things are going wrong or a substitute for taking action to make your circumstances more conducive to joy. If you feel totally stuck, meditate. Study Reiki. Take a hot bath. Give yourself the soothing you need, without food.

Food is about health. Rewards are time to yourself, a nice novel, a walk in the park, quiet time with an appreciative spouse, smiling at the animals at the zoo, telling your dog about your day, asking your cat for stock tips, yoga in the sunshine, a trip to a sunny (or rainy, each to their own Paradise) place, a talking book, a massage and did I mention time to yourself? Life should be a delicious adventure. Make it so.

Recipe 83: Dessert Parfait

Ingredients: about a cup (a small amount) of whole grain, low-sugar cereal; sliced berries or small berries like blueberries (they can be fresh or frozen); plain yogurt; cinnamon.

Here's how it goes:
1. Grab a tallish, cylindrical cup. A coffee mug will do in a pinch, but taller and thinner works better.
2. Layer the cereal thinly but cover the entire bottom for at least ¼ inch.
3. Now add the berries in another equivalent layer.
4. Add the yogurt.
5. Sprinkle cinnamon on the yogurt. Cardamom works well too.
6. Add additional layers of berries and yogurt to fill the glass.
7. Sprinkle psyllium, oat bran or other fiber-adders to the mix, with the cereal or the yogurt.

This has protein from the yogurt and more protein plus good fiber from the cereal and some good stuff from the berries. For dessert, lean more on the yogurt and less on the carbs of the cereal.

Recipe 84: High Protein Pumpkin Pie

Ingredients:
- 2 low-fat graham crusts
- 1 can pumpkin pie mix
- Protein powder, Vanilla (any quality, low-sugar brand; soy, whey)
- 2-4 egg substitutes (they come in containers of 2 eggs each)
- Soy milk, vanilla. [You want something creamy and the nut/rice milks don't really do it. If you have to avoid soy, go with the substitutes. Otherwise, stick to soy.]
- Ground Cinnamon

Here's how it goes:

1. Preheat oven to 425F.
2. Mix pie mix with an equal amount of protein powder.
3. Add 2-4 egg substitutes (more eggs gives a more "custardy" result)
4. Add soy milk until the mixture is moist (amount will vary depending on how many egg subs you used).
5. Add 2 tbs cinnamon.
6. Mix thoroughly.

7. Spoon into crusts, add more cinnamon on top.
8. Bake for 10 minutes, then drop temp to 375 and bake until knife comes out clean.

9. Cool and serve.

May be refrigerated for up to 5 days.

Recipe 85: Lassi, Skyr and other Ethnic Delights With High Protein and Low Sugar/Fat

These can be produced yourself, but only one can be done in 5 minutes.

A **lassi** is an Indian yogurt drink. Take mango non-fat yogurt, add some diet lemon-lime soda, mix it up and have a blissful taste treat. Or if you have been very healthy and abstemious all week – be honest, now! – you can take yourself off to your local Indian restaurant, order vegetables with basmati rice and wash it down with a mango lassi.

Skyr is Icelandic yogurt. The only nationally-available one is Siggi's. This is naturally high in protein, very thick and creamy, low in sugar, flavored with natural sources and completely divine. Don't have more than one/day, but if you can find it, this is a real treat.

Recipe 86: Nut Butter and Celery

Ingredients: a nut butter with the lowest calorie and fat numbers you can find. Try some almond, hazelnut and other types of butters before you reach for peanut. You might be very agreeably surprised at what you can find. Celery. Optional: whole grain crackers.

Here's the complete procedure:

1. Cut celery pieces that are small enough to handle easily, but not so short that they are hard to pick up.
2. Using an ordinary table knife (not too sharp, in other words), pick up gobs of nut butter and fill in the hollow of the celery. Don't let the butter rise above the level of the celery. Fill it in and clear away the extra.
3. Microwave a cup of soup (see soup section – no creamy soups with this recipe), and settle in to crunch your celery.
4. Eat it slowly and savor it.
5. *The slower you eat fats, the less food you will eat and the more satisfying it is.* Fats take much longer to digest than any other kind of food so they help your blood sugar stay stabilized over a longer time. They spread out the value of a meal, in contrast to simple carbs that give you a big shot of sugar and then overstimulate insulin production, leading to a crash.

Recipe 87: A Hollow with Filling

Ingredients: half a cantaloupe or other melon. Plain yogurt. Cinnamon. Vanilla flavoring. Optional: chopped fruit, walnuts.

Here is the complete procedure:

1. Cut a melon in half. Fill the two halves as described. Don't have a friend to eat the other half? Cover the unused half and you have tomorrow's dessert half done.
2. In a small bowl, mix plain yogurt, Vanilla flavoring and a handful of chopped berries, applies, cranberries or other fruit, or walnuts.
3. Spoon the mixture into the cantaloupe.
4. Sprinkle cinnamon heavily on top.

Dig in with a large spoon. Yum!

Recipe 88: Fruit Pie, #1

A normal recipe calls for way too much sugar and fat. This is an option that many people like. It will take more than 5 minutes the first time, because you have to check in a few times until you determine when to intervene. Subsequent iterations will be much quicker and easier!

Ingredients: Jello mix. Finely chopped fruit. Optional: non-dairy topping and sprinkles.

Here's the complete procedure:

1. Chop apples, berries, cranberries and other fruits.
2. Follow the Jello instructions and put the Jello into whole-grain graham cracker crusts.
3. Add the sprinkles. Just a bit, not the whole container!
4. Add the fruits to the Jello after it has had a change to gel a bit. Around 15% of the total set time. This is a bit tricky. You can add it immediately, but you'll likely end up with all the fruit at the bottom. If you wait too long, you'll have fruit only at the top (that's Fruit Pie #2). You want to have a gel that resists your pushing the fruit in, but not too much. The goal is to have the fruit completely covered by the Jello.
5. Put it back and let it finish setting.
6. Serve when ready.

If you use the sugar-free Jello, the calories are low and the fruit is healthy.

You can add a circle of topping around the edge and it doesn't add too much sugar.

Recipe 89: Fruit Pie, #2

Ingredients: Jello mix. Finely chopped fruit. Optional: non-dairy topping and sprinkles. [You thought I was a spoil-sport? Nah.]

Here's the complete procedure:

1. Chop apples, berries, cranberries and other fruits.
2. Follow the Jello instructions and put the Jello into whole-grain graham cracker crusts.
3. Add the sprinkles. Just a bit, not the whole container!
4. Add the fruits to the Jello when it is 60-75% of the way through the total "setting" time. You want to put your fruits in, tightly packed as a top layer, with the almost-set gel holding it in place.
5. Chill and serve.

If you use the sugar-free Jello, the calories are low and the fruit is healthy.

You can add a circle of topping around the edge and it doesn't add too much sugar.

101 Healthy Meals

Recipe 90: High-Protein Muffins

Version 1: Carrots, shredded
Version 2: All-Bran or another very high fiber cereal
Version 3: Berries
Version 4: Creamy

Ingredients vary with the versions above. 2 egg whites or egg substitutes. [Real eggs have too much cholesterol. You can use one whole egg and one egg white.] Milk, either skim or a nut or grain-based milk. Protein powder, preferably vanilla or unflavored. [Use a product based on whey that has no or very little added sugar.] Butter substitute or olive oil spray. A muffin tin. Possibly paper muffin cups if you don't want to oil the muffin tin. Cinnamon.

Here is the complete procedure:

1. Start with a commercial muffin or cornbread mix. The healthy stuff is the best, but with this recipe you can use anything. [The reason we start with a commercial mix is that it contains the "rising" agent, which you would otherwise have to add manually and know how much to add. Too much work for me. This is the cheating way.]
2. Preheat your oven to whatever the package says. I can vary from 350 to 425F.
3. Add Vanilla protein powder to equal the amount of the commercial mix.
4. Add the eggs and mix thoroughly.
5. Is it still dry? Add a SMALL amount of milk and mix. Don't let it get too runny. If you over-hydrate, add a little more protein powder.
6. Add your ingredients, for the versions above. You can experiment.
    a. You can mix carrots and bran, for example.
    b. Berries need to be small. If you have ginormous strawberries, chop them up or buy them sliced.
    c. Creamy means yogurt. If you choose this option, you will be adding more liquid to your mix, unless it is Greek yogurt. Don't add any milk! Add the yogurt, mix it up and see if you need more liquid. I predict you won't. Be generous with the yogurt for a creamy muffin.
7. Grease your muffin tin(s). Use olive-oil based butter substitute on your fingers and grease the interior of the muffin spaces. Or spray olive oil, making sure that you do a thorough job. Or use paper cups. The cups are best if you are doing this for someone other than yourself, as it is more sanitary to grab a muffin by the paper cup.
8. Spoon (don't pour – if you can pour, it is too liquid) the batter into the cups, about 2/3 to ¾ full. Don't fill them to the top; they will rise and expand. You can bake a whole batch in the oven. Sprinkle with cinnamon.
9. Bake as the package instructions suggest. If you have a lot of muffins baking, they may need a few more minutes.

10. Check them by slicing in with a sharp, clean knife. If the knife comes out with sticky goo, it's not ready. If it comes out relatively clean, it is. A topping of golden brown is also a clue.

Get out the olive-oil based spread and enjoy one. They can be frozen and thawed as needed.

One caveat: they are really delicious and they are high in protein, but they can also add up to "too much" if you're not careful. Just eat one per day, unless you are training for a triathlon or eating very abstemiously otherwise. Be honest.

Pie Variant

I have also poured this mixture into a graham cracker crust and made a muffin-pie out of it. Make sure that you don't over-fill.

What if it's a bomb?

The first time you do this, it will likely be overly-dry or overly-liquid. Don't despair. It's just a data point in your culinary experiment. Adjust your amounts next time and get another data point. If you overshot in the other direction, then you have bracketed Perfection and can zero in next time.

Section 6:

All the Stuff That Doesn't Fit in the Other Categories…. Including Seasonal Holiday Dishes

In many ways, this is my favorite category. In it, you will find small meals and snacks, ideas for the major holidays, salads, dips and quite a few things that another author would have put under another category. It probably makes sense in some households to group foods under Lunch, Dinner, Snacks. The reason I didn't? In my experience, people don't conform to the traditional categories any more. Way too many people skip meals or eat a "bar" and call it a meal. What would they search for under Lunch?

For people who are changing to a healthier lifestyle, smaller meals more frequently makes more sense than the older "three squares." The smaller meals in this section are a way to vary the cuisine.

There are some Seasonal Holiday favorites under Section 3 (Vegetables) also.

Recipe 91: Nachos

Version 1: Bare (veggie)

Ingredients: sliced zucchini, cheese sub or low-fat mozzarella.

Here's how it goes:

1. Slice the zucchini (or whatever veggie) thin.
2. Lay them on a microwave plate so that the slices completely cover the plate.
3. Lay cheese to cover every surface.
4. Use sweet spices.
5. Microwave for 60-90 seconds, depending on your machine.

Version 2: Meaty & Veggie Nachos

Ingredients: sliced zucchini, cheese sub or low-fat mozzarella, fake ground round.

Here's how it goes:

1. Slice the zucchini (or whatever veggie) thin.
2. Lay them on a microwave plate so that the slices completely cover the plate.
3. Lay cheese to cover every surface.
4. Layer ground round.
5. Use sweet spices.
6. Microwave for 60-90 seconds, depending on your machine.

This really isn't a full meal.

Add:
- Spinach salad with (of course) walnuts, berries and sliced oranges, plus
- Yogurt sauce, and cinnamon.
- Or oil and vinegar and eat the yogurt separately.
- This is a lot of dairy in one meal so lay off the dairy for 24 hours.

101 Healthy Meals

Recipe 92: Cracker Nachos

Version 1: Veggie

Ingredients: low-fat, low-sugar, cracked wheat, no salt crackers; cheese sub or low-fat mozzarella; kale or Swiss chard.

Here's how it goes:

1. Lay crackers on a microwave plate so that the slices completely cover the plate.
2. Add slices of veggies.
3. Lay cheese to cover every surface.
4. Use sweet spices.
5. Microwave for 60-90 seconds, depending on your machine.

This could be a full meal if it's lunch. If you can, add: Spinach salad with (of course) walnuts, berries and sliced oranges, plus

- Yogurt sauce, and cinnamon. [This is a lot of dairy in one meal so lay off the dairy for 24 hours.]
- Or oil and vinegar

Version 2: Add vegetarian ground round

1. Add a dollop of the ground round to each slice, or just dump it down.
2. Microwave for 60-90 seconds, depending on your machine.

Recipe 93: Acorn Squash with Yogurt and Peppers: Not Just For Holidays!

1. Bake the squash at 350F for about 20 minutes.
2. While that's cooking, microwave sliced peppers (green, yellow, etc.) for about 3 minutes, in water.
3. When the oven timer dings, come back and slice the now-soft squash in half, lengthwise. If you pick it up, you can probably figure out lengthwise; if you don't get it this time, you will next time!
4. Some people throw out the insides. But the seeds and etc. are very nutritious! You might want to at least save the seeds.
5. Put them back in the glass baking dish with water, open side up for another 20-25 minutes.
6. Ding! Pull them out, and put the peppers and plain yogurt with cinnamon and nutmeg in their centers. If you saved the seeds and/or the rest, mix them in.
7. Bake for a final 5-10 minutes.

Recipe 94: Veggies & Vegetarian Chicken, Chorizo, Italian Sausage, etc.

Ingredients: Mixed veggies, like peas and carrots, not just one type of veggie. You can use seafood, cooked, like fake crab meat or smoked wild-caught salmon in the recipe in Section 3: Vegetables. Here we use one of the gazillion types of vegetarian "chicken." Many have excellent taste and are well-spiced. Try different grocery stores!

Option 1: Microwave

1. Get your fresh chopped (nuke about 2 minutes) or frozen chopped veggies (could be 3-4) and follow the microwave directions; my times are estimates and some veggies need more or less.
2. Microwave your chicken until it's warm.
3. Mix together in a bowl.
4. Add one of these: oil & vinegar, especially the spray type, with sweet spices sprinkled on; olive oil based butter substitute with sweet spices; olive oil and Romano cheese; olive oil and Daiya non-dairy cheese.

Options 2-3 are popular for when you have a 2nd chef, especially if someone loves to broil or grill. Or I want to get done faster, because I don't have two microwaves so I can't work the two streams simultaneously!

Option 2: Microwave and broil/bake
1. You can microwave the frozen veggies while you broil or bake the veggie chicken (or veggie chorizo, Italian or other sausage) in a countertop broiler.
2. Toss them together in a bowl.
3. Add one of these: oil & vinegar, especially the spray type, with sweet spices sprinkled on; olive oil based butter substitute with sweet spices; olive oil and Romano cheese; olive oil and Daiya non-dairy cheese

Option3: Microwave and grill
1. You can microwave the veggies while you grill the "meat" outdoors in your grill.
2. Toss them together in a bowl.
3. Add one of these: oil & vinegar, especially the spray type, with sweet spices sprinkled on; olive oil based butter substitute with sweet spices; olive oil and Romano cheese; olive oil and Daiya non-dairy cheese

Recipe 95: Hummus

This is a painless way to get veggies and protein, with good fats and some carbs and fiber. Experiment with all the variations, for quick small meals.

Version 1: Hummus and Veggies
1. Chop up your favorite crunchy veggies. Look at colored peppers (red, green, orange, yellow), celery, broccoli and cauliflower (take Bean-O with these latter two). Some people use fruit, but veggie flavor works better and you need more veggies in your diet.
2. Dip some (not a ton – some) hummus onto your veggie and eat it. With ten or fewer dips, it's not excessively high in calories or fat.

Version 2: Hummus and Whole-Grain Crackers

In addition to, or instead of, veggies, you can use whole grain crackers. Limit yourself to six or fewer. Be really careful about crackers. They may have too much salt, fat, sugar or calories. See what higher-fiber grain crackers you can get at a health food store.

Version 2: Hummus and Pita Slices

Whole wheat pita, sliced into wedges (looks like pizza slices) is the traditional way to scoop some hummus.

Making Your Own Hummus

Hummus is just mashed up garbanzos (chickpeas), mixed with olive oil (you knew there was going to be olive oil here somewhere, right?), lemon juice and parsley. It's healthier than store-bought, but it takes a few minutes. Do it on the weekend. Organize the kids to do the weekend chores, make yourself some hummus and veggies and pita and then take a nice hot soak in the tub with your favorite escapist literature.

Recipe 96: Open-Face Sandwiches

Ingredients: Whole-grain bread; ground-round substitute (plain or Mexican flavor) (find them in any grocery store). Pre-sliced veggies like mushrooms.

Options: pasta sauce; cheese substitute.

1. Toast your bread or leave it untoasted.
2. Microwave the meat substitute with the veggies on top, with or without pasta sauce.
3. Cover the bread with meat substitute/veggie combo. [Alternate: nuke the mushrooms separately and layer them artistically on the meat mix now.]
4. Cheese option: sprinkle cheese or cheese substitute like Daiya (plant protein) on your sandwiches and microwave for another 30 seconds.

Get out your fork and dig in!

Recipe 97: Steamed Veggies

Nobody wants to eat steamed veggies. They want veggies with gravy and sauce dripping all over them. You know why. But in fairness, I have to say that ordinary steamed veggies ARE boring.

So – don't be boring!

1> Chop up those veggies, stick them in the steamer,
2> put water in a sauce pan, set it on high heat and let the veggies cook with just the steam.
3> When they are done, put them in a big mixing bowl, spray them with olive oil spray and dose them with sweet spices.
4> If you have a grill or a microwave, give them another 30 seconds to get the spices into the veggies

….. and I dare anyone to say they are boring.

Recipe 98:   Seafood/Protein Salad

Version 1: Seafood

Ingredients: salad-size shrimp, crab and fake crab (a type of fish) meat. Optionally, clams or leftover fish. Apples. Cranberries. Walnuts.

1. Fill a salad bowl with spinach, chard, kale and other quality greens. No iceberg lettuce.
2. Chop up your apples and add them. Add a handful of cranberries. Two handfuls of walnuts.
3. Add your seafood.
4. Drizzle olive oil and vinegar. Add sweet spices and salt substitutes.
5. Toss.

Forget the croutons. Get some good carbs with whole-grain crackers. This also works well with a cup of lentil soup. Visit the Soup chapter (2).

Version 2: Protein Salad

Ingredients: meat substitute (anything except ground round – fake turkey, chicken, sausage) or actual meat. Quality greens. Walnuts. Optional: cranberries and other chopped fruit.

1. Fill a big salad bowl with spinach, kale, chard and other quality greens.
2. Add your microwaved protein.
3. Add walnuts and chopped fruits.
4. Sprinkle olive oil and vinegar. Toss.

Eat with soup or quality whole-grain crackers.

Recipe 99: Squash, Mashed

This is your basic root-vegetable recipe. Try buying different kinds of squashes. This will take more than 5 minutes the first time you do it.

Ingredients: squash, any type except spaghetti; olive-oil-based butter substitute; sweet spices.

1. Preheat your oven to whatever the label for your squash says. Temp and baking times vary by squash type.
2. Put your squash in a glass baking dish with about ½ inch of water for 20 minutes.
3. Now it should be ready to be sliced in half. Put the halves back to bake for the rest of the time. If the veggie doesn't come with a cooking label, then assume something between 30-45 minutes at 350F. Check it every 8 minutes. When it seems like it's soft enough for mashing…
4. Scrape the interior out into a large mixing bowl. I like to leave the seeds in, as they are a tasty source of protein. Give it a try or serve the seeds separately. [Seeds: Broil them with olive oil spray for 10 minutes.]
5. Mash the innards with a large fork or specialized masher, mixing in a moderate amount of the butter substitute and a generous amount of the spices.

Resist the siren call of gravy. Your taste buds will consider this scrumptious soon. Trust me.

Recipe 100 :   A New View of Fall and Winter Holiday Dinners

- Bake your root veggies with Benecol or other olive oil based condiments, along with sweet spices and plain yogurt. Stay away from butter, sour cream and guacamole.
- Focus on whole-grain side dishes like vegetable biryani or pilaf.
- Consider Tofurkey in addition to turkey. There are complete kits that include all components of the roast, and you can also buy just the "bird." Give it a try – no fat or cholesterol, with plenty of taste and protein.
- Add chopped up tropical fruits for a non-seasonal reminder that summer will come again if we're just patient, that all-American virtue. [Not, but I wish it were.] Mangos have a nice tang that goes well with the traditional harvest root crops.

Have you tried: Sweet Potatoes & Yams? [Some recipes in Vegetables]

Sweet potatoes have lots more vitamins than brown potatoes. Try different options.

Sometimes I cut them up and boil them.
Sometimes I cut them up and microwave them.
Sometimes I cut them up and bake them.

You can serve the slices cooked and chilled overnight, then served with a yogurt and spice dipping sauce.

You can mash them and serve with olive-oil based butter substitute, just like in the squash recipe in this section.

Just don't eat them candied! This is an excellent source of vitamins, minerals and fiber if you don't turn it into a platform for your sugar addiction. Remember: dessert in SMALL quantities.

The laws of thermodynamics still apply and your body still only runs on nutrition, even on Christmas, Thanksgiving and New Years, and even when relatives and friends are nagging or guilt-tripping you – confusing love with candied yams, and more concerned with their ego than with your untimely death. Think like a politician; decide what your talking point will be when offered something you know you will regret - doctor's orders is an oldie but goodie – and keep repeating it, over and over and over, with a smile. They will eventually quit and let you make your own unmolested choices.

101 Healthy Meals

Recipe 101: Eating Out (with a plan)

Bring a small notebook, your private journal – anything that you can write reams on!

If you are a partial or complete vegetarian, and if you are not, it doesn't matter; this research works best if you aim for healthy, non-fried, not-smothered-in-sauces cuisine:

- Search online for a new vegetarian restaurant that you've never been in. Ethnic cuisines sometimes are a good place to explore. Indian cuisine is entirely or mostly vegetarian.

- Explore the dishes that are the lowest in fat, salt, sugar. Ask the server to help.

- Take notes. Look at ingredients, how they are prepared, what vegetables are eaten together. Check out grains you've never heard of. Ask questions. You can ask nearly anything, if you do it with a smile and in a pleasant tone of voice. People are afraid of giving offense with questions – but offense is largely tone of voice, not content. Sound fascinated, not challenging or critical or worried. I can make queries about fat and salt sound like an invitation to the Prince's ball; you can, too. Practice makes perfect!

- Come home and try things!

Moving on From 5 Minute Health

The glory of being a 5 minute gourmet is that you keep your body well-nourished with the highest-quality (meaning, healthiest) fuel possible, for a long and disease-free life. There is NO law that says that we can't have fun within that playground. Explore. Try things. Beware of back-sliding into bad habits, but be on the lookout for new ideas, new vegetables, new spices, new ingredients, new ways of preparing good healthy food without fat, salt and sugar.

Now that you know that eating is about health, what about those rewards? What have you been telling yourself that you can't have?

- Why can't you go to Paris if you really want to and the family as a whole has the money? What would you be willing to give up to afford it? Really think about this. If your family really loves you, they will be willing to sacrifice some of their luxuries to give you something that really matters. If they aren't, then you know something about them and your place in their heart that you didn't before, and knowledge is always powerful. Maybe your days as the only one who sacrifices for others needs to come to an end, so everyone can learn what love means and what a balance of power means.

- Creative endeavors, from painting to crochet to building birdhouses to creating mosaics activates energy centers all through your body. In scientific terms, your brain creates new neurons from neural stem cells when you create. It improves your mental health, your physical health, your joy, your longevity and your wisdom. My book <u>Journey Out of SAD</u> has many good ideas. You don't need to have winter depression to benefit from these ideas. You can get it in print form or Kindle form from Amazon.

- Improve your peace of mind with meditation, yoga and Reiki. See my two books <u>Journey Out of SAD</u> and <u>Take Back Your Lost Heart</u>.

- How about a reward that involves moving? My town has a community pool with a big water slide. Once a week, I reward myself with a lap swim session and then ten or more slides down that glorious slide. Wahoo! Take the kids and the dog for walks. Take your spouse for a session on that water slide or an exploration of a nature park you've never been, while the grandparents or the nice neighbors watch the rugrats.

What you eat, how much you move, using Reiki to give yourself calm and stress relief – these are not separate elements. They are components of the whole tapestry that is your life. Don't let it get snarled. Don't let it unravel. Focus on the tapestry that you are weaving every day. Know that every single thing that you do to help any part of the tapestry makes the whole cloth stronger. Anything that lets down your highest ideals for yourself weakens the whole fabric.

Happy weaving!

Notes

Meet the Author

Victoria Leo (in red, above) has been telling people how to have to live happier and healthier lives for over forty years, but she only started charging for it fifteen years ago, when she completed her Life Coach certification, with a focus on integrated life/health/career. She has a Master's degree in biological anthropology [think Bones] and 2nd MA in Psych, with certifications in Usui Reiki energy healing [Master/Teacher level], Karuna Reiki [Master/Teacher]; clinical hypnotherapy; Past Life regression; intuitive readings and chakra clearing. Victoria has taught in industry, in city and county government, with individuals through her company **Soar With the Eagles**, and at universities, where she has a reputation as a dedicated prof and a tough grader.

Victoria offers a unique blend of techniques and services, focused on exactly what YOU need, not the technique du jour or what is trendy. Visit her at www.soaringreiki.com. You can also find her and her various books on Facebook, and on LinkedIn. Victoria's previous books Take Back Your Lost Heart: A Toolkit for Living with Courage and Caring in the Turbulent 21st

Century and Journey Out of SAD: Beat the Seasonal Blues NOW! are available on Amazon. The latter is available on Kindle as well.

Victoria shares her home in the Pacific Northwest with a herd of three cats and two house rabbits, an engineer who develops new ways to attach decals to jumbo-jets, and a cell phone that has really bad reception and doesn't do anything except make phone calls. She keeps her calendar in pencil but she does own a Kindle and does cool stuff with audio and video, so she's not actually a Luddite.

Services:
> **Reiki Energy Healing**
> **Intuitive Readings: Goddess, Angel, Animal Guides**
> **Past Life Regressions**
> **Life Coaching to find your best job or spiritual path**
> **Chakra clearing**

> **Classes:**
   * **Reiki Levels I/II/III (Usui Master); Karuna I/II/III (Master)**
   * **Specialized Reiki classes for nurses, therapists, Creatives**
   * **Creative Chakras (for creativity)**
   * **Human Biology for Everyone (CDs and live classes)**

Soar With the Eagles, 17300 SE 270th Place #9102, Covington WA 98042

www.soaringreiki.com
http://reikitrainingfornurses.com
www.linkedin.com/victorialeo

An interview with the Author

(recorded Q&A with a health coaching client)

Q: Where did you get your recipes? What other books can we buy to find them?

A: *I don't own cookbooks. I hate to cook. People like me don't own cookbooks and pore over recipes. I love people. I love getting together with them. If only I could convince my church, my team, my group-du-jour to meet at a restaurant instead of having a potluck. Yeah, I know a potluck saves money and it allows all the cooks out there to strut their fat/sugar/salt stuff. For me, it's just a nightmare. My simple Get It Nutritious & Git 'Er Done stuff does not translate into wanting to cook a big batch for others. So I tend to make a pumpkin pie – or buy something – and sit down with the gang and eat as little as possible (the healthy stuff of which there's usually just a green salad, no protein) or I eat at home earlier. Did I mention I hate cooking but I love eating and I love health?*

The way I developed my recipes is the way I love to experience life: I experimented. At the end of two decades, I had a mental encyclopedia of stuff I loved to eat and could whip up in 5 minutes of prep. Millions of failed experiments were just data points on the road to getting it from Won't Kill You *to* Yeah, It's Edible *to* All Right!

Q. Why did you decide to write it all down? Why now and not earlier? Or never?

Two things pushed me to commit my brain-dump to paper. I married a wonderful man who was amenable to our keeping a no-meat home, but found that he had no idea what to cook that wasn't the four meat dishes that he had been living on. [Married men live longer, healthier lives than single guys. One reason is that a woman drags them to doctors and makes them find cancers when they are small and curable, and makes them prevent diabetes, strokes and heart disease. Another reason is that a woman cooks more than four dishes, so they get food variety and usually healthier diets.] I talked him through several dishes, but he's an engineer and therefore prefers following procedures and protocols. So he needed a written copy.

And so did my clients. So much of my work these days is health coaching, and most of my clients are trying to improve their health by eating better – but they don't know what to eat or how to prepare it. Clearly, having a book that they could consult would be a great boost to their success. There are many healthy eating cookbooks and vegetarian cookbooks, but not so many quick-and-healthy low-meat or no-meat cookbooks. So there was a motivation to help my clients.

I also know quite a number of very fine cooks who own a lot of cookbooks who would occasionally ask me for a recipe. Of course, I had nothing written down to give them, so I would scribble directions on a napkin and they would lose it. No surprise there. Even people who don't have Smart Phones know that that is not an efficient way to share information!

Q: Is this the complete contents of your brain, the entire canon in V?

No. It's just the most elementary 101. I have another 50 that I had to cull out to keep it at 101, which is a cool number. Perhaps a second book titled <u>And 50 More!</u> Maybe some stuff for people who are willing to invest TEN whole minutes in prep. I do know a couple of dozen of those, really cool stuff. But I don't know, would people be willing to spend ten whole minutes??

Q: It's possible. Keep writing them down!

SPECIAL OFFER FOR 101 READERS

To help you kick-start some healthy eating and living, call for a free 20 minute Health Coaching session!

Call 253-203-6676.

Receipt not required, but be prepared to share where you bought this, or where the gifter bought it.

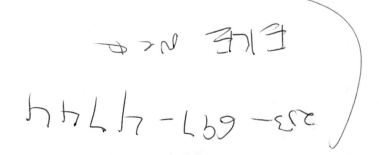